McGRAW-HILL READING

Practice

Grade K

Pupil Edition

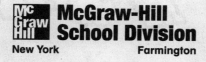

**McGraw-Hill
School Division**

New York   Farmington

CONTENTS

Unit 2: ALL KINDS OF FRIENDS

We Fit!

The Tan Cat

Unit 3: TIME TO SHINE

That Tam!

Nat Is My Cat

On the Dot

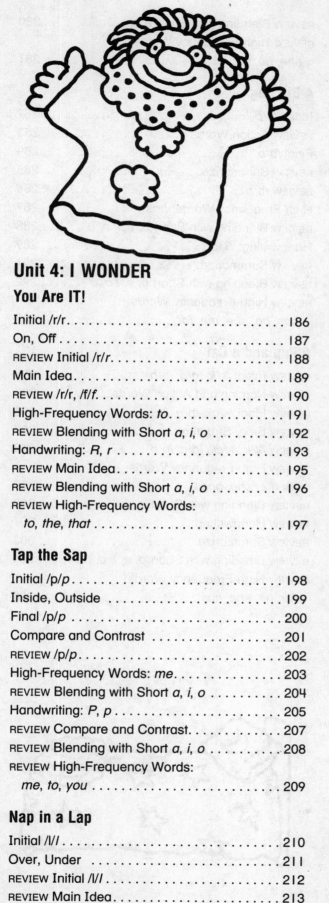

Unit 4: I WONDER

You Are IT!

Tap the Sap

Nap in a Lap

Mud Fun

Fun in the Sun

Unit 5: LET'S WORK IT OUT

Unit 6: CHOICES

Hop with a Hog

We Win!

The Vet Van

Jen and Yip

Zack and Jan

Name _____

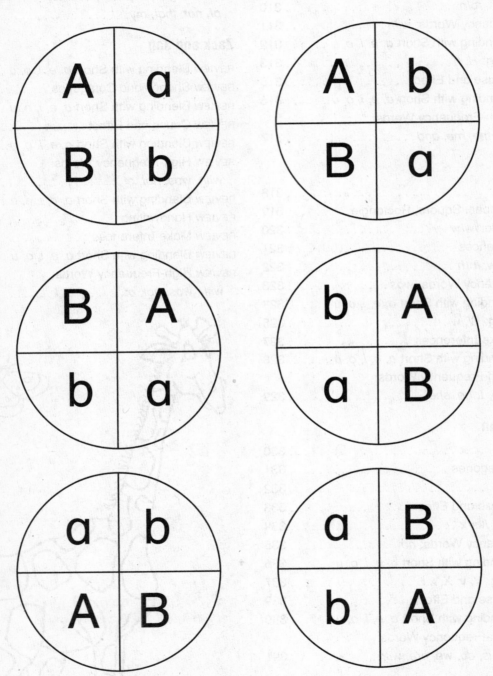

Find the two sets of capital and lowercase letters in each circle. Color the shapes with *A* and *a* in one color. Color the shapes with *B* and *b* in a second color.

At Home: Take turns finding words on cereal boxes with the letters *A, a, B,* or *b*.

Unit 1
Introduce *Aa, Bb* 12

Name _____

Draw a line from left to right to connect the person with the place where he or she is going.

4 Unit 1
Introduce Left to Right

At Home: Read a story to the child, running your finger along the text from left to right as you read.

Name _____

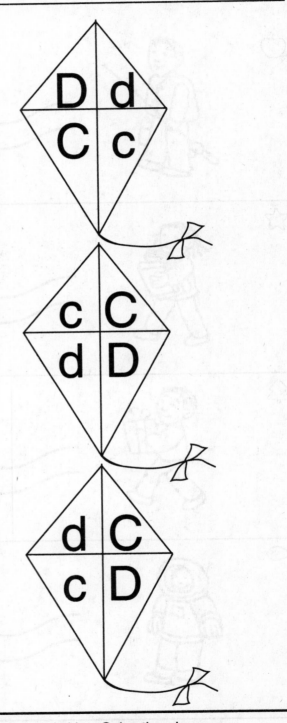

Find the two sets of capital and lowercase letters in each kite. Color the shapes with *C* and *c* in one color. Color the shapes with *D* and *d* in a second color.

At Home: At the supermarket, see how many products or brand names with *C*, *c*, *D*, or *d* you both can find.

Unit 1
Introduce *Cc, Dd* **12**

Name _____

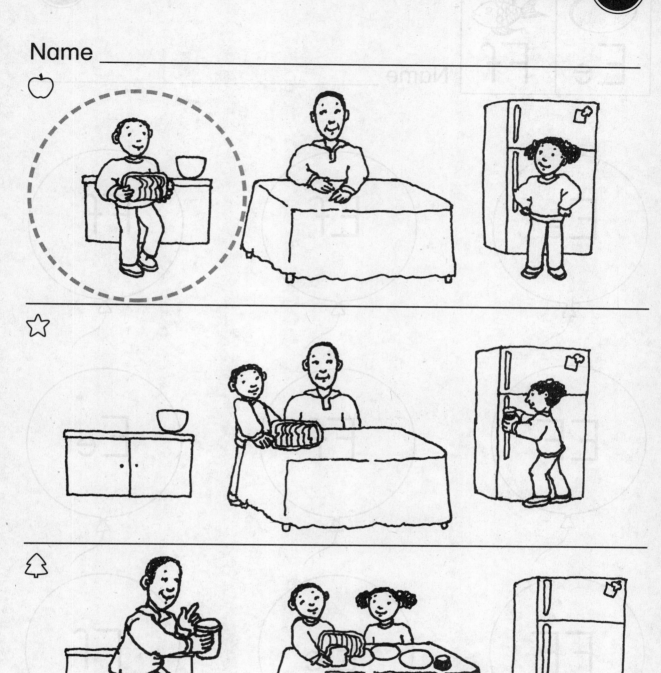

Ask children to look at the picture. Then read the sentences aloud. ⏺ *At lunchtime, Tyler got out bread to make a sandwich. Draw a circle around Tyler.* ☆ *Laura went to the refrigerator to get some jelly. Draw a circle around Laura.* 🌲 *Dad said, "Don't forget the peanut butter." Draw a circle around Dad.*

Unit 1
Introduce Use Illustrations

At Home: Look at pictures with the child. Together, point to and name some of the things you see.

Name _____

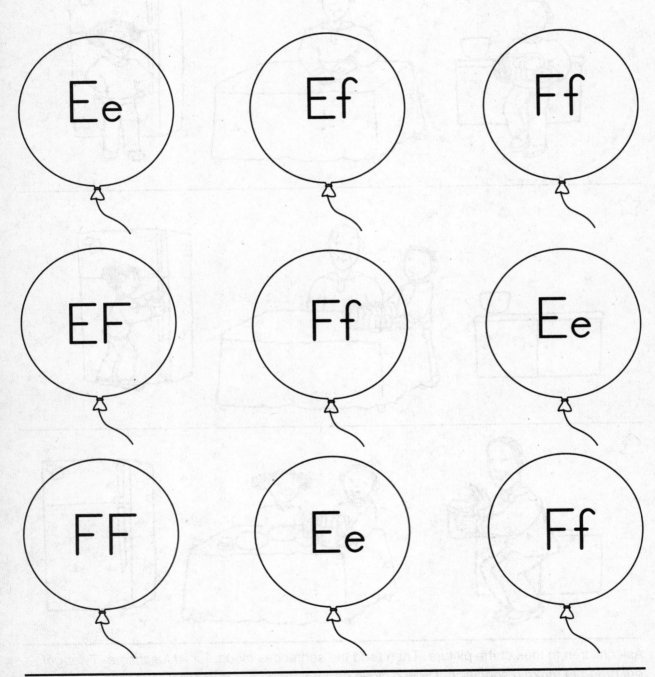

Color only those balloons that have the capital and lowercase forms of the same letter.

Name _____

the

---

the

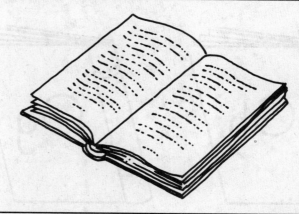

---

the

 ☆ Say the word and picture name. Draw a circle around the word *the*. △ Draw a picture of something in your classroom after the word *the*. Then draw a circle around the word *the*.

4 Unit 1
Introduce High-Frequency Words: *the*

At Home: Take turns pointing to various things in the room. Have the child say aloud, "the _____" for each one.

Gg | Hh

Name _____

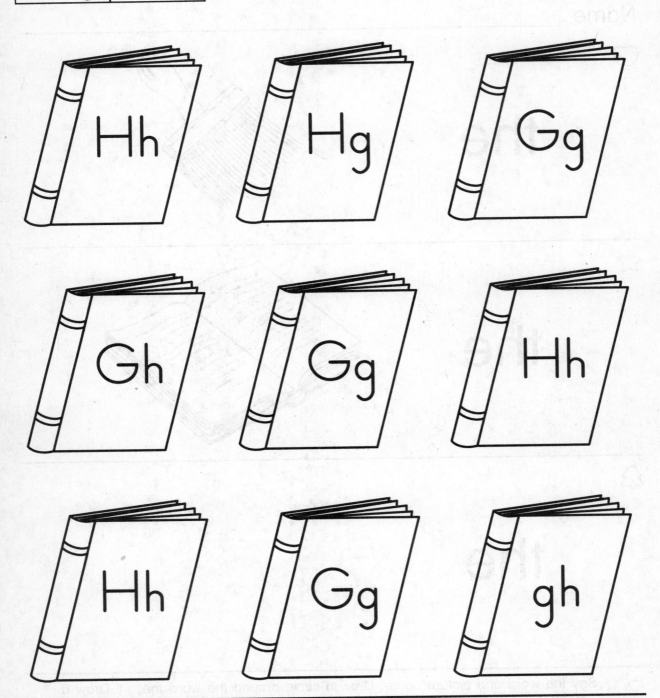

Color only those books that have the capital and lowercase forms of the same letter.

At Home: At the library or at home, browse together through books for words with *G*, *g*, *H*, or *h*.

Unit 1
Introduce *Gg*, *Hh*
9

Name _____

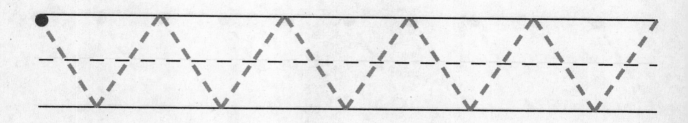

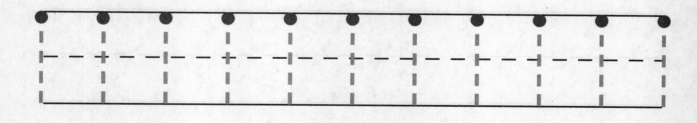

Trace and write the lines. Start at the dot.

4 Unit 1
Handwriting Readiness

At Home: Draw two parallel lines about an inch apart.
Take turns writing lines that stay within those two lines.

Name _____

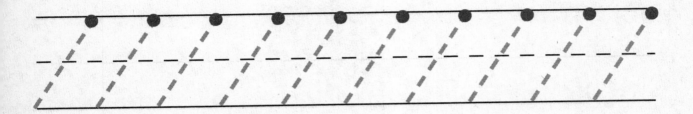

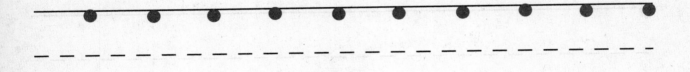

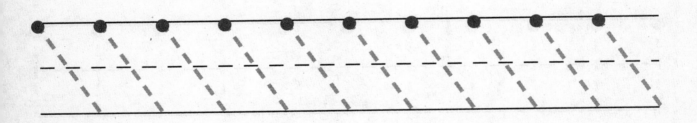

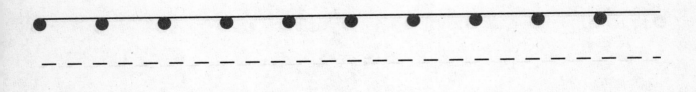

Trace and write the lines. Start at the dot.

At Home: Line up a group of utensils, such as forks, slanting to the left. Have the child change their position to all slant to the right and then to all stand straight up.

Unit 1
Handwriting Readiness

4

McGraw-Hill School Division

14

Name _____

Ask children to look at the picture. Then read the sentences aloud. 🍎 *Shiro has a new bike.*
Draw a circle around Shiro. ☆ *Amy watched him learn to ride. Draw a circle around Amy.*
🌲 *Dad said, "You're doing just fine." Draw a circle around Dad.*

Unit 1
Review Use Illustrations

At Home: Look at pictures with the child. Take turns
pointing to and naming things you see.

Ii Jj Kk

Name _____

Find all the socks that have the capital and lowercase forms for the same letter. Color the socks with *I* and *i* in one color. Color the socks with *J* and *j* in a second color. Color the socks with *K* and *k* in a third color.

At Home: In red, write capital letters *A–K* as the child says the letters. In blue, do the same for lowercase letters *a–k*.

Unit 1
Introduce *Ii, Jj, Kk*

 12

Name _____

the

☆

the

🌲

the

🍎 ☆ Say the word and picture name. Draw a circle around the word *the*. 🌲 Draw a picture of something in your kitchen. Then draw a circle around the word *the*.

Unit 1
Review *the*

At Home: Together, name objects in your kitchen using the word *the*. Draw and label several objects using *the*.

Name _____

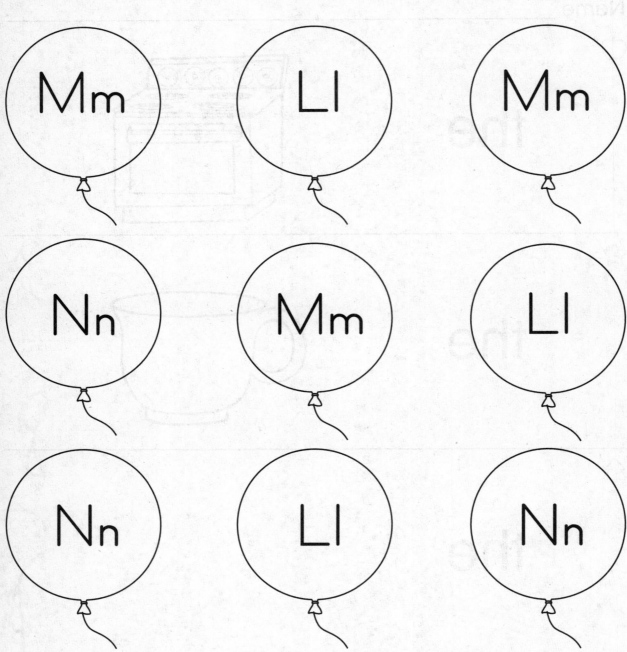

Find all the balloons that have the capital and lowercase forms for the same letter. Color the balloons with *L* and *l* in one color. Color the balloons with *M* and *m* in a second color. Color the balloons with *N* and *n* in a third color.

At Home: Make two sets of letter cards with the letters *L*, *l*, *M*, *m*, *N*, and *n*. Play "Concentration" with the child by finding matching capital and lowercase letters.

Unit 1
Introduce *Ll, Mm, Nn*

9

Name _____

Draw a circle around the *first* animal in each row. Draw a line under the *next* animal in each row. Color the *last* animal in each row.

Unit 1
Introduce First, Next, Last

At Home: Have the child pick three small items; arrange them in a row; and tell which is first, next, and last.

Name _____

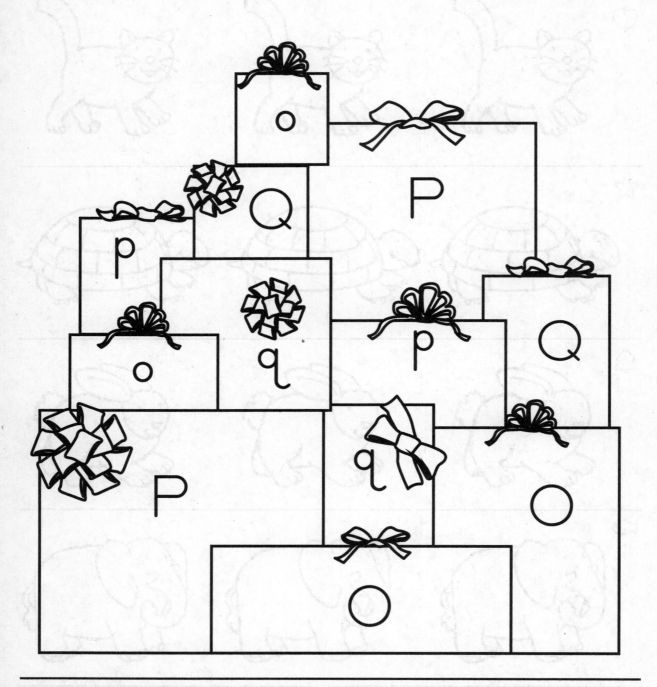

Find all the presents that have the capital and lowercase forms for the same letter. Color the presents with *O* and *o* in one color. Color the presents with *P* and *p* in a second color. Color the presents with *Q* and *q* in a third color.

At Home: Keep tallies of things that begin with *O, o, P, p, Q,* or *q.* Which tally is longest? Shortest?

Unit 1
Introduce *Oo, Pp, Qq*

Name _____

Look at the pictures in each box. Draw a circle around the picture that shows what happened first. Draw a line under the picture that shows what happened next.

Unit 1
Introduce Sequence of Events

At Home: Name two things that happen each morning.
Discuss which happens first and which happens next.

Rr | Ss | Tt

Name _____

Find all the socks that have the capital and lowercase forms for the same letter. Color the socks with *R* and *r* in one color. Color the socks with *S* and *s* in a second color. Color the socks with *T* and *t* in a third color.

At Home: Write the letters *R, r, S, s,* and *T, t* randomly on a piece of paper. Ask the child to draw a line from the capital to the lowercase form of each letter.

Unit 1
Introduce *Rr, Ss, Tt* | 12

McGraw-Hill School Division

Name _____

a

☆

a

🌲

a

---

a

🍎 ☆ 🌲 Say each word and picture name. Draw a circle around the word *a*.

🐟 Draw a picture of something that has wheels after the word *a*. Then draw a circle around the word *a*.

4 Unit 1
Introduce High-Frequency Words: *a*

At Home: Take a walk together and point out vehicles.
Have the child say, "a _____" aloud for each one.

Name _____

Find all the balloons that have the capital and lowercase forms of the same letter. Color the balloons with *U* and *u* in one color. Color the balloons with *V* and *v* in a second color. Color the balloons with *W* and *w* in a third color.

At Home: Read a favorite story together. Find words and names with *U, u, V, v, W,* and *w.*

Unit 1
Introduce *Uu, Vv, Ww*

Name _____

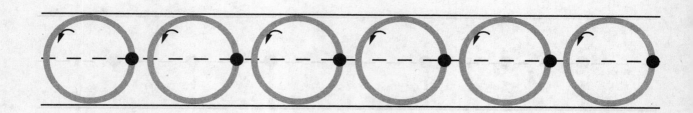

Trace and write the circles. Start at the dot. Follow the direction of the arrow.

McGraw-Hill School Division

4 Unit 1
Handwriting Readiness

At Home: Use a brush dipped in water and a brown paper bag. Together, make a circle from left to right and then a circle from right to left.

25

Name _____

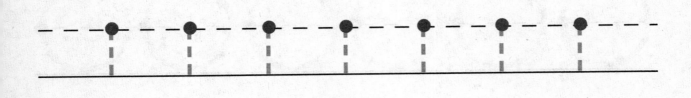

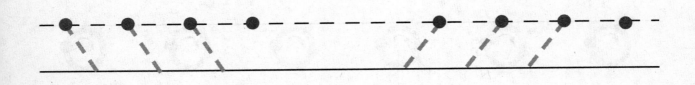

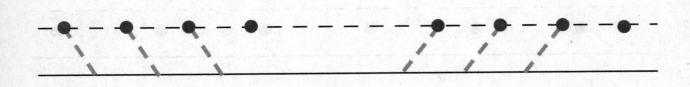

Trace and write the lines. Start at the dot.

At Home: Use several long straws and as many short straws. Line the long straws up all slanting to the left. Have the child line the short straws up the same way. Repeat with slanting to the right and then straight up.

Unit 1
Handwriting Readiness

McGraw-Hill School Division

Name _____

Look at the pictures in each box. Draw a circle around the picture that shows what happened first. Draw a line under the picture that shows what happened next.

Unit 1
Review Sequence of Events

At Home: Take turns acting out two different actions. Ask, "What happened first?" "What happened next?"

Name _____

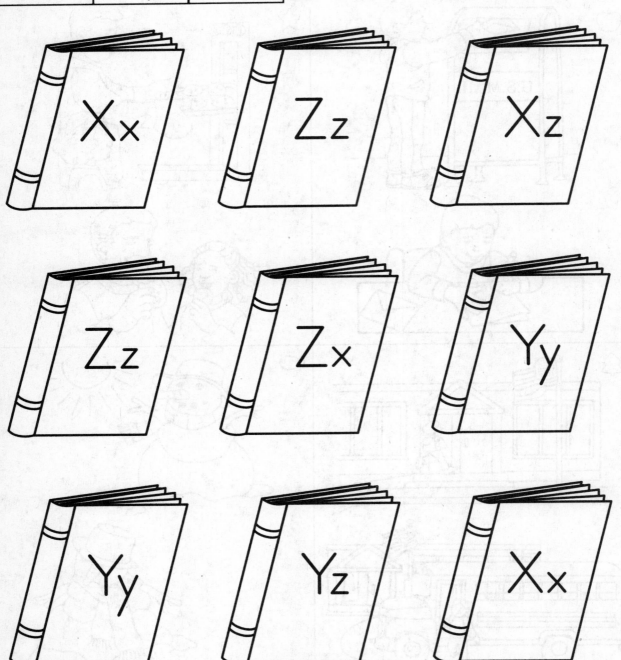

Find all the books that have the capital and lowercase forms of the same letter. Color the books with *X* and *x* in one color. Color the books with *Y* and *y* in a second color. Color the books with *Z* and *z* in a third color.

At Home: Together, try to find the complete alphabet on auto license plates you see during one day.

Unit 1
Introduce *Xx, Yy, Zz* 9

Name _____

the	a (the)
a	a the
the	the a

Say the word at the beginning of each row. Draw a circle around the word where you see it in the same row.

McGraw-Hill School Division

3 Unit 1
Review a, the

Nn Name _____

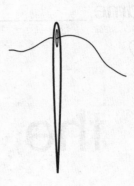

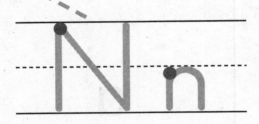

Trace the letters *Nn*. Say the word that names each picture. Color each picture whose name begins with the same sound as *nest*, and draw a line from these pictures to the letters *Nn*.

At Home: Look at a calendar. Have the child find the month that begins with *N* and pictures whose names begin with *n*.

Unit 1
Introduce Initial /n/n 9

Name _____

○ Take out your red crayon. Color the pictures red. ☆ Take out your yellow crayon. Color the pictures yellow. ♤ Take out your blue crayon. Color the pictures blue.

Unit 1
Introduce Colors

At Home: Take turns looking around the room and naming things that are red, yellow, or blue.

_n   Name _____

n

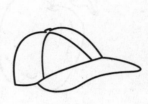

Say the name of each picture. Write the letter *n* under each picture that has the same ending sound as *fan*.

At Home: Play "Rhyme Time." Have the child think of words that rhyme with *ten* and *hen*. Emphasize the ending sound.

Unit 1
Introduce Final /n/ *n*

6

Name _____

  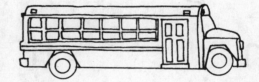

Look at the picture at the top. ○ Color the picture that shows what kind of weather it is. ☆ Color the picture that shows how the children get to school. ♧ Color the picture that shows what the children are wearing. ◁ Color the picture that shows what animal is on the leash.

 Unit 1
Review Use Illustrations

At Home: Look at a picture together and make up a story. Pick out things from the picture that help tell the story.

Nn __n Name _____

Say the name of the picture. Where do you hear the sound /n/*n*? Draw a circle around the first *n* to show if it is the beginning sound (as in *nest*). Draw a circle around the second *n* to show if it is the ending sound (as in *fan*).

At Home: Decide together which color names end with /n/ (*tan*, *brown*, *green*). Find examples of each color on food packages.

Unit 1
Review /n/*n* 6

Name _____

my

☆

my

△

my

○ ☆ Say the word and picture name. Draw a circle around the word *my*. △ Draw a picture of something you play with after the word *my*. Then draw a circle around the word *my*.

3 Unit 1
Introduce High-Frequency Words: *my*

At Home: Have the child draw a picture of his or her room. Help the child label the picture "My Room" and describe the items in the picture.

McGraw-Hill School Division

Name _____

🍎

N H Z Ⓝ

☆

b b d p

🌲

G Q G C

Look at the first letter in each row. Circle the same letter each time you see it in the same row. Use a different color for each row.

At Home: Together, choose three letters. After you write them, the child uses a different color to circle the capital and lowercase forms of the same letter.

Unit 1
Review Letter Identification

9

N n

Name _____

Trace and write capital *N*. Start at the dot.

Unit 1
Handwriting: *N*

At Home: Together, practice writing two or more names
that begin with *N*, such as *Nancy*, *Nicholas*, *Nora*, or *Neil*.

Nn

Name _____

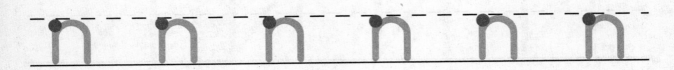

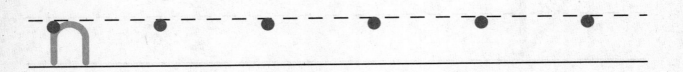

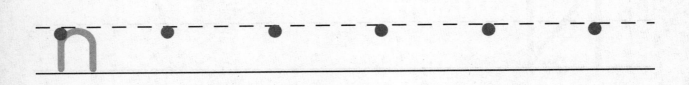

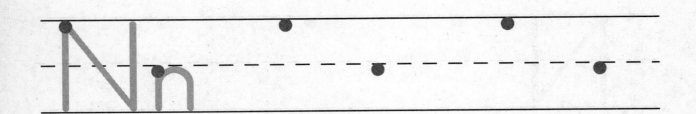

Trace and write lowercase *n*. Start at the dot. On the last line, trace and write *Nn*.

At Home: As you both practice writing *Nn*, notice that capital *N* has all straight lines, while lowercase *n* has a curved line.

Unit 1
Handwriting: N, n
4

McGraw-Hill School Division

Name _____

 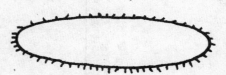

 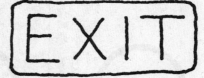

Look at the picture of the classroom. ○ Color the picture that shows where the children are sitting. ☆ Color the picture that shows who is teaching the class. ♧ Color the picture that shows a sign in the classroom. ↪ Color the picture that shows what is on the shelves.

8 Unit 1
Review Use Illustrations

At Home: Take turns pointing out parts of a picture from a book or magazine. Describe some details.

Name _____

🍎

W | V N  W

☆

r | r f v

🌲

Q | G D Q

Look at the first letter in each row. Circle the same letter each time you see it in the same row. Use a different color for each row.

At Home: Write a mixture of capital and lowercase letters on paper. Ask the child to use one color to circle the capital forms, another color for the lowercase ones.

Unit 1
Review Letter Identification | 9

40

Name _____

a

the

my

the

Say the word and picture name. Draw a circle around the word in front of the picture.

4 Unit 1
Review *my, the, a*

At Home: Have the child point to an object and say *a, the,* or *my* before saying its name. Repeat with other objects.

Name _____

 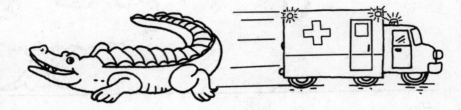

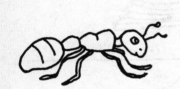 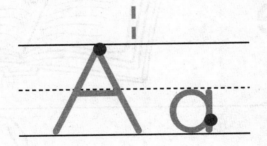 

Trace the letters *Aa*. Say the word that names each picture. Color each picture whose name begins with the same sound as *apple*, and draw a line from these pictures to the letters *Aa*.

At Home: Together look for the word *at* in a newspaper and circle it.

Unit 1
Introduce Initial /a/a
9

Name _____

 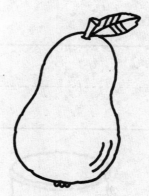 

⟳ Take out your green crayon. Color each item in the row green. ☆ Take out your orange crayon. Color each item in the row orange. ♤ Take out your purple crayon. Color each item in the row purple.

9 Unit 1
Review Colors

At Home: Have the child draw a picture of his or her favorite fruits. Then name the color of each fruit and have the child color each fruit.

_a_

Name _____

a a

Write the letter _a_. Say the word that names each picture. Listen for the sound in the middle of the word. Color each picture whose name has the same middle sound as _cat_.

At Home: Write the letter _a_ and take turns putting a letter on either side to make a word.

Unit 1
Introduce Medial _a_   9

Name _____

Draw a circle around the picture that shows what happened first. Draw a line under the picture that shows what happened next. Color the picture that shows what happened last.

9 Unit 1
Review Sequence of Events

At Home: Prepare a meal together. Choose a dish and follow a recipe, noting the order of each step.

Name _____

 a   a   a   a

a   a   a   a   a   a

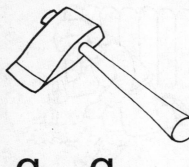  

a   a   a   a   a   a

Say the name of the picture. Where do you hear the sound /a/a? Draw a circle around the first *a* if it is the beginning sound (as in *apple*). Draw a circle around the second *a* if it is the middle sound (as in *cat*).

At Home: Make several *Aa* and _ *a* _ letter cards. Mix the cards and pick one. The child says a word using /a/a as on the card.

Unit 1
Review /a/a   9

Name _____

that

☆

that

🌲

that

🍎 ☆ Say the word and picture name. Draw a circle around the word *that*. 🌲 Draw a picture of an animal after the word *that*. Then draw a circle around the word *that*.

Unit 1
Introduce High-Frequency Words: *that*

At Home: Put objects in a paper bag. Have the child feel one object without looking and say, "I feel *that* ____." If the child guesses the object correctly, give him or her an index card with the word *that* written on it.

Name _____

a	n

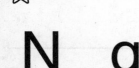

a n

a n

N a n

N a n

Say the sound each letter at the top of the page stands for. Blend the sounds to say the word. Say the name of the picture that comes after the word. Trace the letters to write the word. Blend the sounds to say the name. Trace the letters to write the name.

At Home: Have the child point to the arrow that goes from *a* to *n* in *an*. Say the word *an* together. Do the same with the arrows and letters in *Nan*. Take turns using *an* and *Nan* in sentences.

Unit 1

Introduce Blending with Short *a*

2

Name _____

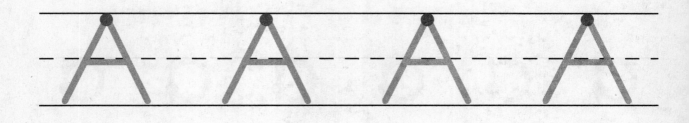

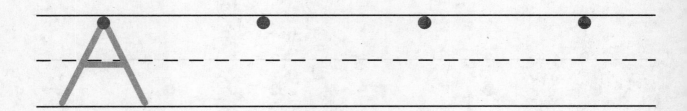

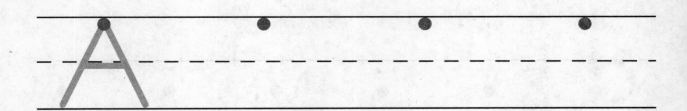

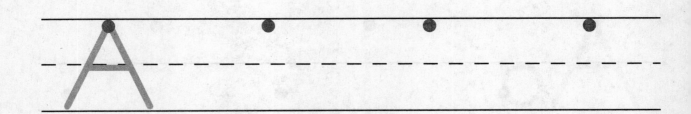

Trace and write capital *A*. Start at the dot.

McGraw-Hill School Division

4 Unit 1
   Handwriting: *A*

At Home: Together, practice writing capital *A* in the air.
Say "Aaron, Adam, Ana" and other names as you do so;
if you wish, help the child write the names.

Aa

Name _____

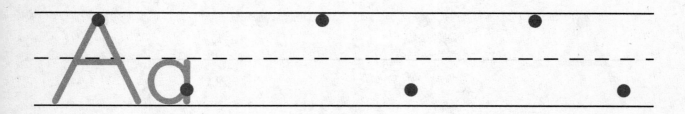

a a a a a a

a   • • • • •

a   • • • • •

Aa

Trace and write lowercase *a*. Start at the dot. On the last line, trace and write *Aa*.

At Home: As you practice these letters together, watch that the child puts the straight line in lowercase *a* on the correct side of the letter.

Unit 1
Handwriting: A, a

4

Name _____

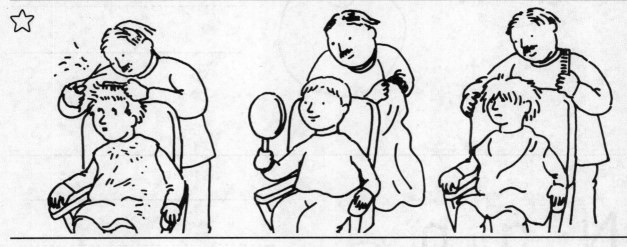

Draw a circle around the picture that shows what happened first. Draw a line under the picture that shows what happened next. Color the picture that shows what happened last.

9

Unit 1
Review Sequence of Events

At Home: Discuss a task the child recently learned.
Tell the steps it takes to perform the task.

Name _____

a	n

 a n

_____
- - - - - - - - - - - -
_____

☆ N a n

_____
- - - - - - - - - - - -
_____

Say the sound each letter at the top of the page stands for. Blend the sounds to say the word. Say the name of the picture that comes after the word. Write the word. ☆ Blend the sounds to say the name. Write the name.

At Home: Have the child point to the arrow that goes from *a* to *n* in *an*. Say the word *an* together. Do the same with the arrows and letters in *Nan*. Take turns using *an* and *Nan* in sentences.

Unit 1
Review Blending with Short *a*

2

Name _____

🍎 a	the 
⭐ my	my that
🌲 the	that the
🐟 that	that my

Say the word at the beginning of each row. Draw a circle around the word where you see it in the same row.

 Unit 1
Review *the, a, my, that*

At Home: Read a story together. Point out examples of *the, a, that,* and *my* to each other.

Name _____

n

a

n

a

n

a

n

a

n

a

n

a

Say the name of each picture. Draw a circle around the letter that stands for the sound you hear at the beginning of each picture name.

At Home: Count together. When you say a number word with /n/, nod your head. Note, number words do not have /a/.

Unit 1
Review Initial /n/n, /a/a

Name _____

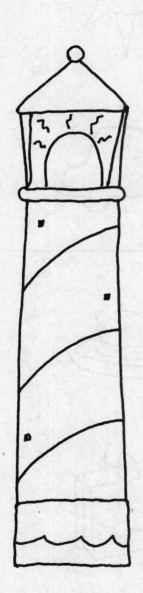 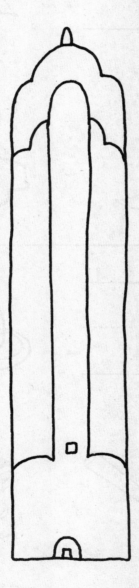 

Look at the building on the left part of the page. Color it red. Color the next building blue. Color the last building green. On the right part of the page, draw another kind of building.

Unit 1
Review Colors; Left to Right;
First, Next, Last

At Home: Look at a bookshelf together. Go from left to right and take turns saying the color of each book cover. Find two that are the same color.

Name _____

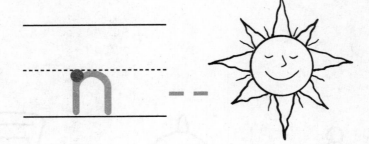

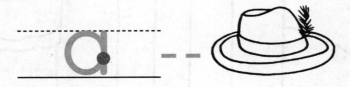

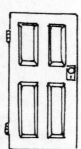

Write the letter *n*. Draw a line from the letter *n* to each picture whose name ends with the same sound as *fan*. ☆ Write the letter *a*. Draw a line to each picture whose name has the same middle sound as *cat*.

At Home: Look at a newspaper together. Help your child find words that end in *n*.

McGraw-Hill School Division

Unit 1
Review Final /n/n, Medial /a/a

Name _____

Look at the picture at the top. ⬭ Color the picture that shows two children playing in the classroom. ☆ Color the picture that shows what the children are painting. ♧ Color the picture that shows who is reading in the classroom. ⇨ Color the picture that shows what animal the children see.

8 Unit 1
Review Use Illustrations

At Home: Take turns looking through magazines or newspapers. Find an interesting picture and tell a story about it.

Name _____

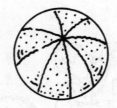
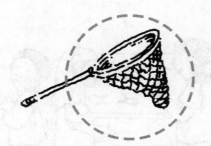

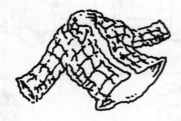

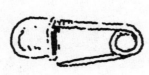

Look at the first picture. ⟳ ☆ Draw a circle around the picture whose name has the same beginning sound. △ Draw a circle around the picture whose name has the same ending sound. ⌒ Draw a circle around the picture whose name has the same middle sound.

At Home: Have the child draw a nest and a sun on two separate index cards. Then say words that have the letter *n*, such as *fan*, *night*, *man*, *no*, and so on. For each word, have the child point to the card that shows whether the /n/ sound is at the beginning or end of the word.

Unit 1
Review /n/n, /a/a

Name _____

🍎 the

☆ a

🌲 that

🐟 my

Say the word and picture name. Draw a circle around the word in front of the picture.

Unit 1
Review *the, a, my, that*

At Home: Point out articles of clothing together. Say
that shirt, my shirt, the coat, a coat, and so on.

Name _____

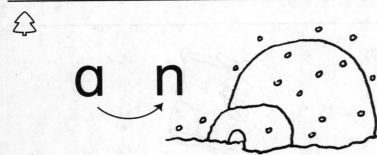

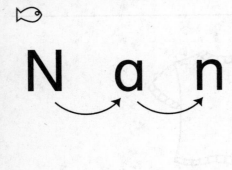 

🍎 ☆ 🌲 Blend the sounds to say the word. Say the name of the picture that comes after the word. Write the word. 🐟 Blend the sounds and say the name. Write the name.

At Home: Write *an*. Take turns saying the sound for *a* and blending it with the sound for *n* to make the word *an*. Use *an* in a sentence.

Unit 1
Review Blending with Short *a*

4

Name _____

a an Nan

A An Nan

Trace the words. Then write the words under their models.

Unit 1
Handwriting Review

At Home: Write *a*, *an*, and *Nan*. Make the capital *A* and *N* twice as high as the lowercase *a* and *n*.

Name _____

Nan Nan a

A an an An

Trace the words. Then write the words under their models.

McGraw-Hill School Division

At Home: Help the child make capital and lowercase *N* and *A* by writing these words in sand with a stick. Talk about which letters are tall.

Unit 1
Handwriting Review 4

Name _____

Draw a circle around the picture that shows what happened first. Draw a line under the picture that shows what happened next. Color the picture that shows what happened last.

12
Unit 1
Review Sequence of Events

At Home: Take turns telling a story. Ask each other what happens first, next, and last in the story.

Name _____

○ _____

a n

☆ _____

♤ _____

⌔ _____

○ Trace the word. Say the word and the picture name. ☆ ♤ Write the word *an* in front of the picture. Say the word and the picture name. ⌔ Write the girl's name that goes with the picture.

At Home: Face the same direction as the child as you both write the word *an* in the air several times. Say the letters as you write.

Unit 1
Review Blending with Short *a*

4

Name _____

the that my

a my that

the that a

a my the

Read the three words in each row. ○ Draw a circle around the word *the*. ☆ Draw a circle around the word *my*. 🌲 Draw a circle around the word *that*. 🐟 Draw a circle around the word *a*.

Unit 1
Review *the*, *a*, *my*, *that*

At Home: List four favorite foods together. The child writes *the*, *a*, *my*, or *that*, you write the food names.

Dd

Name _____

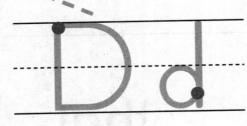

Trace the letters *Dd*. Say the word that names each picture. Color each picture whose name begins with the same sound as *duck*. Draw a line from these pictures to the letters *Dd*.

At Home: Take turns finding words that begin with *D* or *d* in storybooks and their titles.

Unit 2
Introduce Initial /d/d
9

Name _____

③ 2	2 4	1 4
5 4	4 2	5 4

Draw a circle around the number that shows the correct number of objects.

 Unit 2
Introduce Numbers

At Home: Together, gather 3 toys, 4 books, 5 forks, and so on.

_ d

Name _____

  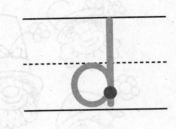

  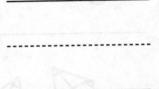

 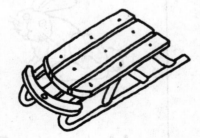

Say the name of the pictures in each row. Color the picture whose name has the same ending sound as *bed*. Write the letter *d*.

At Home: Write *sad* and read it together. Change *s* to *d* to form a new word. Then change *dad* to *mad*.

Unit 2
Introduce Final /d/d 6

Name _____

Think about the story "Warthogs in the Kitchen." In each row, draw a circle around the picture or pictures that show something from the story.

9 Unit 2
Introduce Story Details

At Home: Read a story aloud as you both look at the pictures. Close the book and take turns retelling one thing that happened in the story.

Name _____

(d)	d	d	d
d	d	d	d
d	d	d	d

Say the name of the picture. Where do you hear the sound /d/*d*? Draw a circle around the first *d* if it is the beginning sound (as in *duck*). Draw a circle around the second *d* if it is the ending sound (as in *bed*).

At Home: Look at an ad in the newspaper together to find words that begin or end with *d*.

Unit 2
Review /d/*d* 6

McGraw-Hill School Division

Name _____

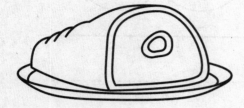 **and**

☆

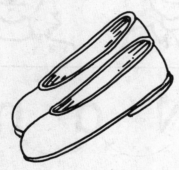 **and**

🌲

 **and**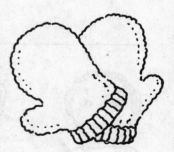

Say the picture names and the word in each row. Draw a line under the word *and*.

3 | Unit 2
Introduce High-Frequency Words: *and*

At Home: Together, think up other combinations of items.
Say them aloud: _____ and _____.

Name _____

🍎 a n

an

⭐ D a n

🌲 D a d

🐟 N a n

🍎 Blend the sounds and say the word. Trace the word. Write the word on the line below it. ⭐ 🌲 🐟 Blend the sounds and say the name. Write the name. Draw a line under the picture that goes with the name.

At Home: Write *an*. Take turns saying the sound for *a* and blending it with the sound for *n* to make the word *an*. Use *an* in a sentence. Do the same for *Dan*, *Dad*, and *Nan*.

Unit 2
Review Blending with Short *a*

Dd Name _____

D D D D

D

D

D

Trace and write capital D. Start at the dot.

Unit 2
Handwriting: *D*

At Home: Together, take a stick and practice writing *D* in the
ground, in the sand, or in another soft surface, such as clay.

McGraw-Hill School Division

Dd Name _____

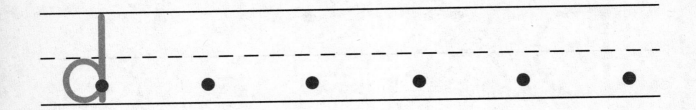

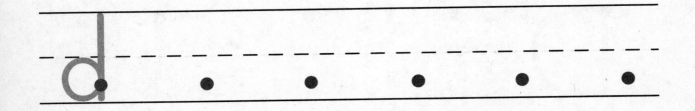

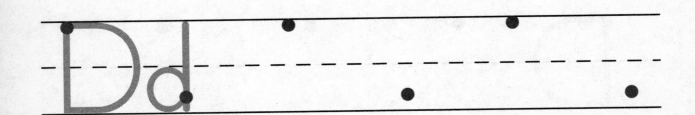

Trace and write lowercase *d*. Start at the dot. On the last line, trace and write *Dd*.

McGraw-Hill School Division

At Home: Practice writing *Dd* together. As you write each letter, take turns saying a word that starts with *D* or *d*: *dog*, *Dad*, *do*, *Dom*, *doll*, *dig*, and so on.

Unit 2
Handwriting: *D*, *d*. 4

Name _____

Think about the story "Dan and Dad." In each row, draw a circle around the picture that shows something from the story.

9 Unit 2
Review Story Details

At Home: Read a story aloud. Then say things that *did* and things that *did not* occur. The child then checks the book to make sure.

Name _____

Dan Nan

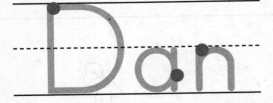

Dad Nan

_____

Dad Nan

_____

Nan Dan

_____

Look at the picture. Read the names. Draw a line under the name that goes with the picture. Write the name.

At Home: Play "Match It." Make two word cards for *an*, *Dan*, *Dad*, and *Nan*. Put the cards facedown and take turns turning them over to make pairs.

Unit 2

Review Blending with Short *a*

 8

McGraw-Hill School Division

Name _____

my  and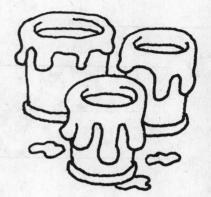

a  and

my and

🍎 ☆ Read each word and say the picture names. Draw a circle around the word *and*. Draw a line under the word *my*. Draw two lines under the word *a*. 🌲 Draw a circle around the word *and*. Draw a line under the word *my*. Draw a picture of two things that belong to you.

3 | Unit 2
Review *and*, *my*, *a*

At Home: Play "Pair Up." You say *a* ___. The child says *and* ___, completing the pair.

Ss Name _____

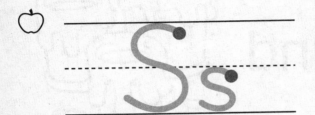

 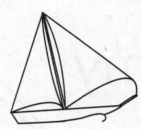

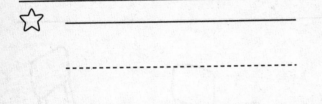

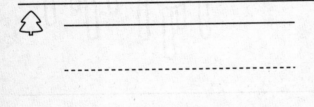

 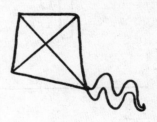

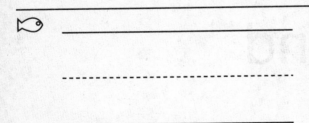

Write the letters *Ss*. Say the word that names each picture. Color the picture whose name begins with the same sound as *sock*.

At Home: Each of you puts your hand in a sock to make a sock puppet. Take turns having the sock say words that begin with *s*.

Unit 2
Introduce Initial /s/s
8

Name _____

 8 9

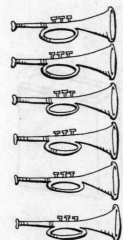 7 6

 9 7

 10 2

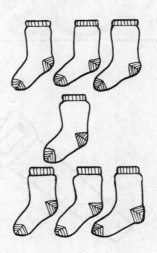 6 7

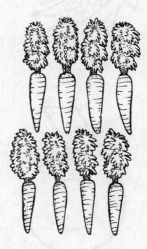 8 10

Draw a circle around the number that shows the correct number of objects.

 6 Unit 2
Review Numbers

At Home: Gather socks in groups of different numbers from 6 to 10. Have the child tell how many are in each group.

Ss Name _____

Trace the letters *Ss.* Say the word that names each picture. Color each picture whose name begins with the same sound as *sock*, and draw a line from these pictures to the letters *Ss.*

At Home: Play "Sock It to Me." Use a pair of rolled-up socks to play catch. Say a word that begins with *s* each time you toss the "ball."

Unit 2
Review Initial */s/s* 9

Name _____

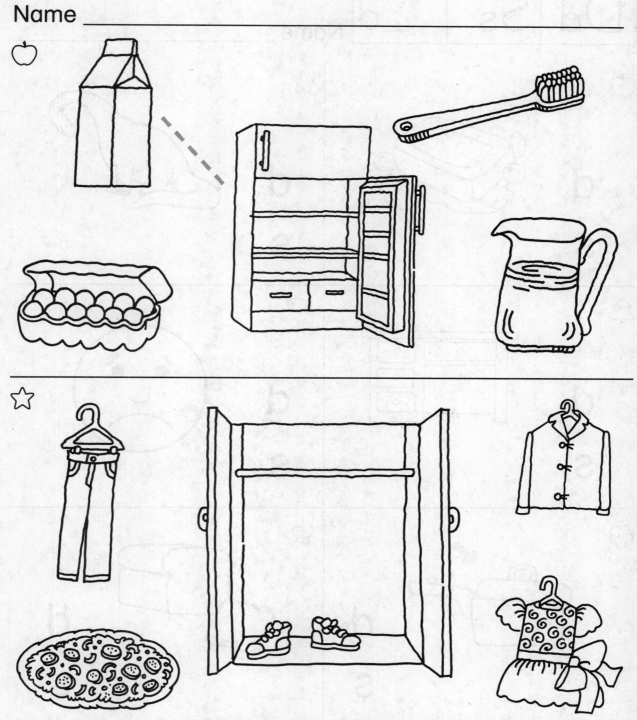

Draw lines to show the three things that belong in the refrigerator. ☆ Draw lines to show the three things that belong in the closet.

8 Unit 2
Introduce Classify and Categorize

At Home: Place several pairs of socks in a pile. Help the child sort them and tell how they are alike.

Name _____

d
s

d
s

d
s

d
s

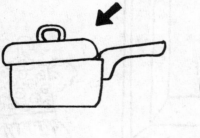

d
s

d
s

☼ ☆ 🔺 🐟 Say the name of each picture. Draw a circle around the letter that stands for the sound you hear at the beginning of each picture name. ✿ 🦋 Say the name of each picture. Draw a circle around the letter that stands for the sound you hear at the end of each picture name.

At Home: Together find words that begin with *d* and *s* in a dictionary. Then see if any of the words end with *d*.

Unit 2
Review /s/s, /d/d

6

McGraw-Hill School Division

Name _____

I   .

I   .

I   .

I   .

Read the sentence by saying the word and telling about the picture. Draw a circle around the word *I*. Draw a picture of yourself doing something to help out after the word *I*. Then draw a circle around the word *I*.

Unit 2
Introduce High-Frequency Words: *I*

At Home: Make a list of things your child does to help out at home. Have your child circle the word *I* and draw a picture of his or her favorite thing to do.

Name _____

 N a n

Nan

D a d

_____

 s a d

_____

_____

D a n

_____

_____

Blend the sounds and say the word. Write the word. Draw a line under the picture that goes with the word.

At Home: Write *Nan*. Take turns saying the sound for *N* and blending it with the sound for *a* and the sound for *n* to make the word *Nan*. Use the word *Nan* in a sentence. Do the same for *Dad*, *sad*, and *Dan*.

Unit 2
Review Blending with Short *a*

84

Name _____

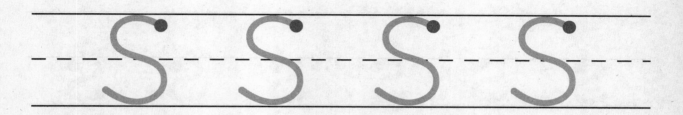

Trace and write capital *S*. Start at the dot.

Unit 2
Handwriting: *S*

At Home: As you write *S* together, try to guide the child to make the upper and lower curves equal.

Ss

Name _____

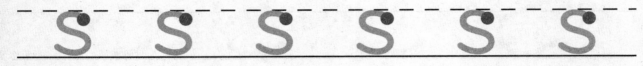

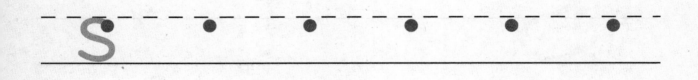

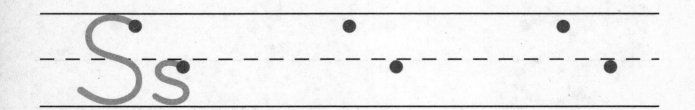

Trace and write lowercase s. Start at the dot. On the last line, trace and write Ss.

At Home: As you practice writing lowercase s together, help the child to see that the letter is half the height of capital S, but otherwise is formed in exactly the same way.

Unit 2
Handwriting: S, s 4

McGraw-Hill School Division

Name _____

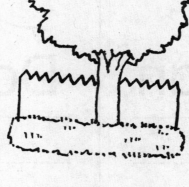

🍎 Draw lines to show the three things that belong in the classroom. ☆ Draw lines to show the three things that belong in the garden.

Unit 2
Review Classify and Categorize

At Home: Play "Categories." Name three things that belong together. Ask your child to name one more.

Name _____

sad   an

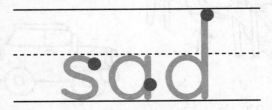

Dad   Dan

Dad   Nan

Dad   sad

Look at the picture. Read the words. Draw a line under the word that goes with the picture. Write the word.

At Home: Add two cards with the word *sad* to your card set of the words *an*, *Dan*, *Dad*, and *Nan*. Use all the cards to make pairs as you play "Match It."

Unit 2
Review Blending with Short *a*

Name _____

 **and**

---

 my  **and**

I  **my** 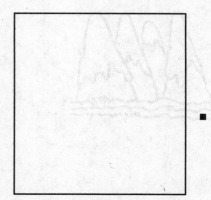 **.**

Say each word and the picture names. ○ ☆ Draw a circle around the word *and*. △ Draw a circle around the word *I*. Next to the word *my* draw a picture of something or someone you love. Then draw a circle around the word *my*.

5 Unit 2
Review *I*, *and*, *my*

At Home: Together, make a card for a relative. Help the child write *I love my* _____. Have your child draw a picture to go with it.

Mm   Name _____

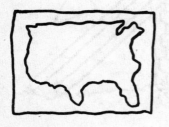

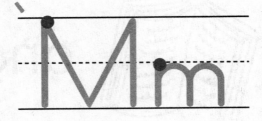

Trace the letters *Mm*. Say the word that names each picture. Color each picture whose name begins with the same sound as *moon*, and draw a line from these pictures to the letters *Mm*.

At Home: Play "Musical Chairs." Walk around chairs singing words that begin with *m*. Sing a word that does not and everyone sits.

Unit 2
Introduce Initial /m/m

9

Name _____

Find the circles in the picture. Color them yellow. Find the triangles in the picture. Color them blue.

Unit 2
Introduce Shapes: Circle, Triangle

At Home: Together, draw and color your own picture. Use circles and triangles and choose one special color for each shape.

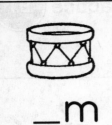

_m

Name _____

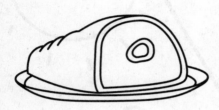

m

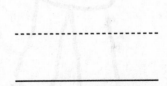

Say the name of each picture. Color the picture whose name has the same ending sound as *drum*. Write the letter *m*.

At Home: Play "Rhyme Time." Take turns. One player says a word that ends with *m*. The other says a rhyming word (for example, *jam, ham*).

Unit 2
Introduce Final /m/m

6

Name _____

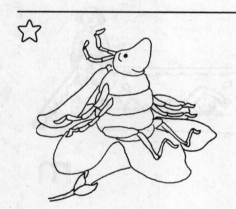

Think about the story "The Chick and the Duckling." In each row, draw a circle around the picture that shows something from the story.

3 Unit 2
Review Story Details

At Home: As you read a story together, take turns asking each other a question about each page. For example, Did _____ happen?

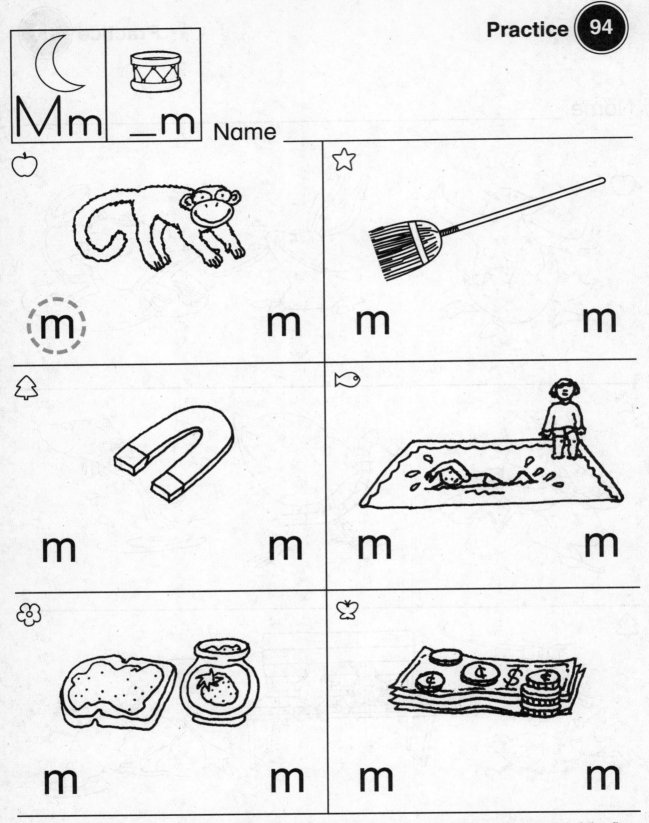

M m   _m   Name _____

m

m   m

m   m   m

m   m   m

Say the name of the picture. Where do you hear the sound /m/m? Draw a circle around the first *m* if it is the beginning sound (as in *moon*). Draw a circle around the second *m* if it is the ending sound (as in *drum*).

At Home: Take turns looking in storybooks for words that begin or end with the letter *m*.

Unit 2
Review /m/m   6

Name _____

A ♡ is  .

A  is 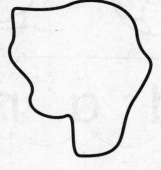 .

A  is 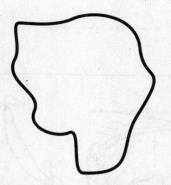 .

🍎 Use your red crayon. Color the two items in the sentence. Read the sentence: *A heart is red.*
☆ Use your yellow crayon. Color the two items in the sentence. Read the sentence: *A banana is yellow.* 🌲 Use your green crayon. Color the two items in the sentence. Read the sentence: *A leaf is green.* Then draw a line under the word *is* in each sentence.

Unit 2
Introduce High-Frequency Words: *is*

At Home: Together, make a "Color Book." Choose other objects and colors to fit into the sentence *A ___ is ___.*

Name _____

🍎
m a n

_____

- - - - - - - - - - - - - - -

m a n

☆
S a m

_____

- - - - - - - - - - - - - - -

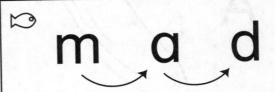

🌲
d a m

_____

- - - - - - - - - - - - - - -

🐟
m a d

_____

- - - - - - - - - - - - - - -

Blend the sounds and say the word. Write the word. Draw a line under the picture that goes with the word.

At Home: Write *man*. Take turns saying the sound for *m* and blending it with the sound for *a* and the sound for *n* to make the word *man*. Use *man* in a sentence. Do the same for *Sam*, *dam*, and *mad*.

Unit 2
Review Blending with Short *a*

  8

Mm

Name _____

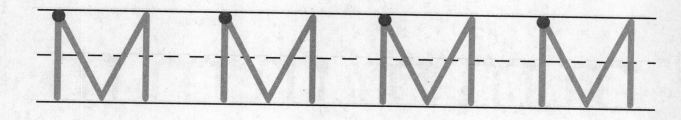

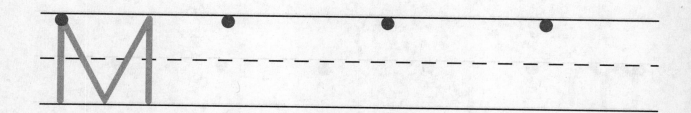

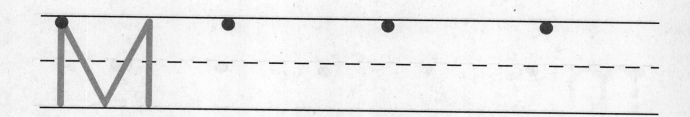

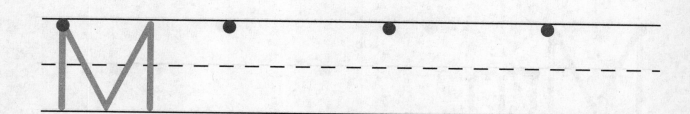

Trace and write capital *M*. Start at the dot.

Unit 2
Handwriting: *M*

At Home: As you both practice capital *M*, pay special attention to the vertical lines and the slanted lines.

Name _____

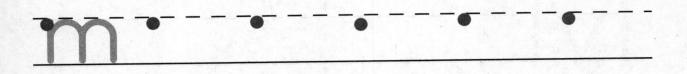

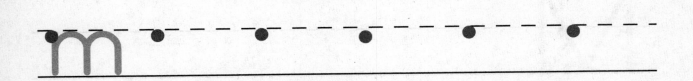

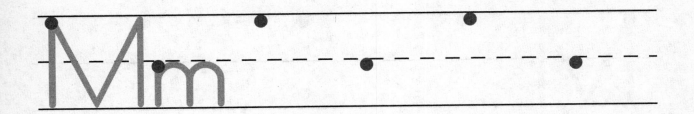

Trace and write lowercase *m*. Start at the dot. On the last line, trace and write *Mm*.

At Home: As you practice writing *Mm*, guide the child to see that capital *M* has sharp angles, while lowercase *m* has curves.

Unit 2
Handwriting: *M, m*

McGraw-Hill School Division

Name _____

🍎

☆

🌲

Think about the story "I Am Sam!" In each row, draw a circle around the picture that shows something from the story.

9 Unit 2
Review Story Details

At Home: After you read a story, describe a story event. Have the child find the page for that part. Take turns describing and finding.

Name _____

mad ham

_____

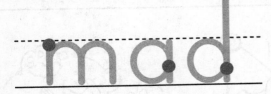

Nan man

_____

- - - - - - - - - -

an sad

_____

- - - - - - - - - -

man mad

_____

- - - - - - - - - -

Look at the picture. Read the words. Draw a line under the word that goes with the picture. Write the word.

At Home: Add two cards each with the words _mad_ and _man_ to your card set of the words _an, Dan, Dad, Nan,_ and _sad_. Use all the cards to make pairs as you play "Match It."

Unit 2
Review Blending with Short _a_

Name _____

that	**and**	**that**
I	**is**	**I**
is	**is**	**a**
and	**that**	**and**

Say the word at the beginning of each row. Draw a circle around the word where you see it in the same row.

Unit 2
Review is, I, and, that

At Home: Write sentences using the above words. Ask the child to circle *that, I, is, and*.

I i

Name _____

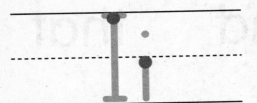  

 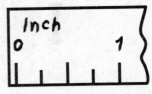

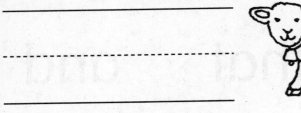  

Write the letters *Ii*. Say the word that names each picture. Color the picture whose name begins with the same sound as *igloo*.

At Home: Play "Itty Bitty Insects." Take turns naming insects that are less than one inch long, such as an ant, a ladybug, and so on.

Unit 2
Introduce Initial /i/i 8

Name _____

Find the squares in the picture. Color them blue. Find the rectangles in the picture. Color them red.

 11 Unit 2
Review Shapes: Square, Rectangle

At Home: Have the child point to squares and rectangles found on floors, on wallpaper, or in other places.

i

Name _____

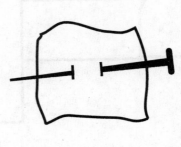

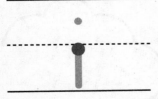

i

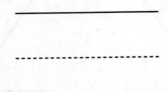

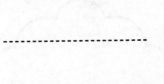

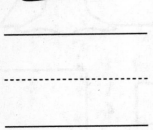

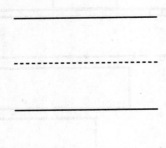

Say the name of each picture. Write the letter *i* under each picture that has the same middle sound as *pig*.

At Home: Use letter cards to form the word *dad*. Together, read the word and then change the *a* to *i* to form a new word.

Unit 2
Introduce Medial /i/i

6

Name _____

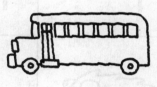

Color the three pictures that belong to the same group.

16 Unit 2
Review Classify and Categorize

At Home: Have the child help you organize kitchen utensils or silverware by categories.

I i   ___ i ___

Name _____

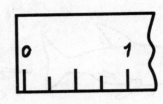

i    i   i   i   i

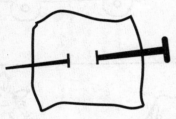

i    i   i   i   i

i    i   i   i   i

Say the name of the picture. Where do you hear the sound /i/i? Draw a circle around the first *i* if it is the beginning sound (as in *igloo*). Draw a circle around the second *i* if it is the middle sound (as in *pig*).

At Home: Find words in books or magazines that rhyme with *pin* (*win*, *tin*) and *sit* (*pit*, *lit*).

Unit 2
Review /i/i
9

McGraw-Hill School Division

Name _____

🍎

Dad said, "Dan!"

⭐

Dan said, "Nan!"

🌲

I said, "Dad!"

Read the sentence. Then draw a line under the word *said*.

Unit 2
Introduce High-Frequency Words: *said*

At Home: Play "Simon Said." Take turns giving the
directions "Simon said ____." Have the child do what
"Simon said"!

Name _____

○ d i d _____

☆ d i m _____

♧ i n _____

⋙ M i n _____

○ ☆ ♧ Look at each word. Blend the sounds and say the word. Write the word. Use the word aloud in a sentence. ⋙ Blend the sounds and say the name. Write the name. Use the name aloud in a sentence.

At Home: Make two sets of letter cards for *d, i, m, M, n*. Have the child build the words above and read them. Then have the child use each word in a sentence.

Unit 2

Introduce Blending with Short *i*

McGraw-Hill School Division

I i

Name _____

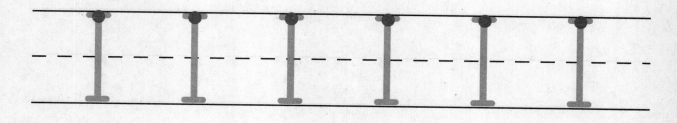

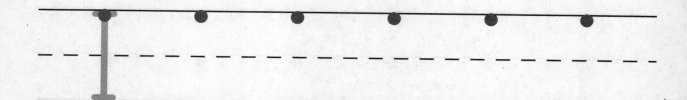

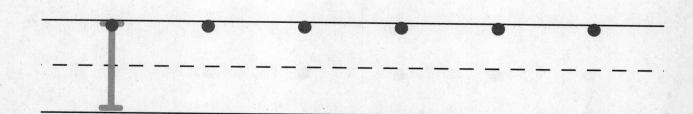

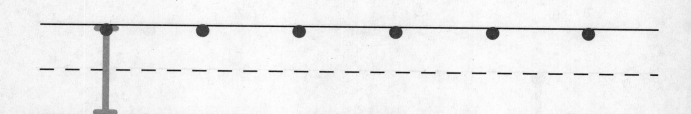

Trace and write capital *I*. Start at the dot.

 Unit 2
Handwriting: *I*

At Home: As you practice writing uppercase *I*, watch that
the child adds the "head" and "foot" to each letter.

Ii

Name _____

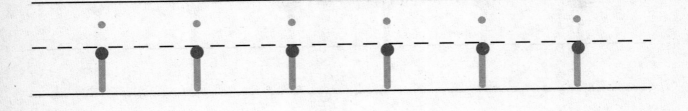

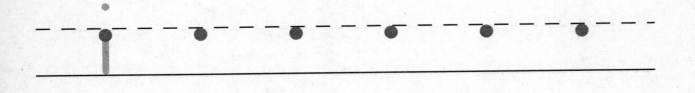

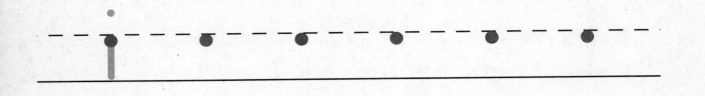

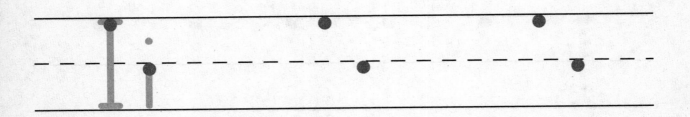

Trace and write lowercase *i*. Start at the dot. On the last line, trace and write *Ii*.

At Home: As you practice *Ii*, be sure that the child puts the dot over lowercase *i*. Say, "Mark the spot ... little *i* gets a dot."

Unit 2
Handwriting: *I*, *i*

Name _____

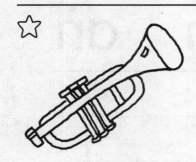 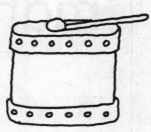  

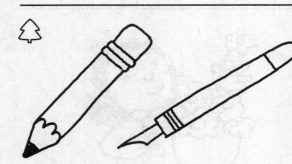  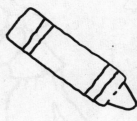

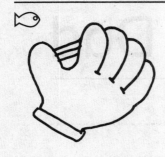 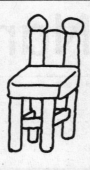 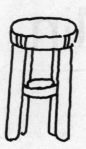 

Color the three pictures that belong to the same group.

16 Unit 2
Review Classify and Categorize

At Home: Put some buttons in a pile and sort them with the child by color, then by size, then by number of holes.

Name _____

in   dim

_____

in

_____

man   an

_____

_____

Dan   Min

_____

_____

Nan   Dad

_____

_____

Look at the picture. Read the words. Draw a line under the word that goes with the picture.
Write the word.

At Home: Write *in* and take turns creating new words by
adding a letter to the left. Read the words together and
use them in a sentence. Do the same for *an*.

Unit 2
Review Blending with Short *i*, *a*

McGraw-Hill School Division

Name _____

⏣	is	in	is
☆	said	said	and
♤	I	A	I
⚲	is	and	is

Say the word at the beginning of each row. Draw a circle around the word where you see it in the same row.

Unit 2
Review *said, I, is,*

At Home: Together, take turns saying words that rhyme with the words *said*, *I*, and *is*. Accept nonsense words, but encourage the child to think of real words.

Name _____

d
s
m

d
s
m

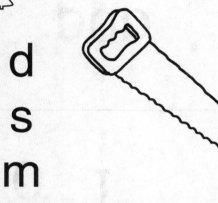

d
s
m

d
s
m

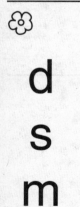

d
s
m

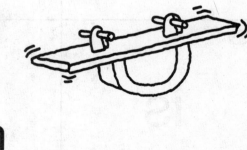

d
s
m

Say the name of each picture. Draw a circle around the letter that stands for the sound you hear at the beginning of each picture name.

At Home: Put several letter cards for *d*, *s*, and *m* facedown. Take turns turning them over and saying a word that begins with the letter.

Unit 2
Review Initial /d/d, /s/s, /m/m
6

Name _____

🍎

5

6

⭐

9

10

🌲

7

8

🍎 Color 6 squares. Draw a circle around the correct number. ⭐ Color 10 triangles. Draw a circle around the correct number. 🌲 Color 8 rectangles. Draw a circle around the correct number.

Unit 2
Review Shapes and Numbers

At Home: Draw 10 circles. Then pick a number from 1 to 10. Ask the child to color that number of circles.

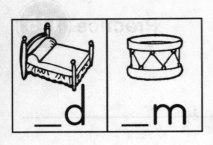

Name _____

Say the name of each picture. Draw a circle around the letter that stands for the sound you hear at the end of each picture name.

McGraw-Hill School Division

At Home: Play "Rhyme Time." Take turns saying words that end with *d* and *m*. The other person says a word that rhymes.

Unit 2
Review Final /d/d, /m/m

6

Name _____

Think about the story "The Chick and the Duckling." In each row, draw a circle around the picture that shows something from the story.

9 Unit 2
Review Story Details

At Home: Play "Prove It." After you read a story, take turns asking questions that require a yes or no answer. One person asks "Can you prove it?" The other finds the page.

Name _____

s d

Say the picture name. Write the letters that stand for the beginning and ending sounds in each picture name.

At Home: Say the word *sad* and write it together. Do the same with *dad*. Note that both words end with the same letter.

Unit 2
Review /d/d, /m/m, /s/s | 8

Name _____

○ I   and   is

☆ and   said   I

🌲 is   and   said

🐟 I   said   and

Read the words. ○ Draw a circle around the word *and*. ☆ Draw a circle around the word *I*.
🌲 Draw a circle around the word *is*. 🐟 Draw a circle around the word *said*.

4 Unit 2
Review *and, I, is, said*

At Home: Take turns writing, saying, and spelling each of
the Review Words.

Name _____

Sam

Min

Sam

Sid

mad

Blend the sounds and say the word. Write the word. Draw a line under the picture that goes with the word.

At Home: Write *id* and ask the child to write a *d* to the left of *id* to create a word. Read the word *did* together and use it in a sentence. Do the same for *ad*, *am*, and *in*.

Unit 2
Review Blending with Short *i*, *a*

Name _____

_____
and is man
_____

_____
_____

I said Sam

_____
_____

_____

Trace the words. Then write the words under their models.

4 Unit 2
Handwriting Review

At Home: Have the child show you how to make a capital
S and how to make a lowercase *s*. How are they the
same? How are they different?

Name _____

Sid am an

Dad did in

Trace the words. Then write the words under their models.

McGraw-Hill School Division

At Home: Have the child show you how to make a capital *D* and how to make a lowercase *d*. How are they different?

Unit 2
Handwriting Review 4

Name _____

  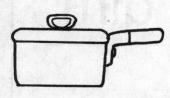 

Color the three pictures that belong to the same group.

16 Unit 2
Review Classify and Categorize

At Home: Have the child help you sort laundry into whites
and colors by type of item (socks, towels, and so on).

Name _____

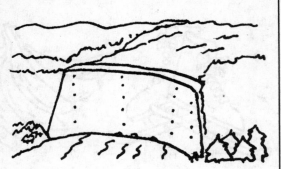

dam dim

_____

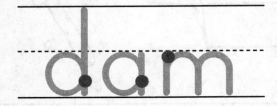

dam

man mad

_____

- - - - - - - - - - - - - - - - - - - -

_____

in   an

_____

- - - - - - - - - - - - - - - - - - - -

_____

Sid sad

_____

- - - - - - - - - - - - - - - - - - - -

_____

Look at the picture. Read the words. Draw a line under the word that goes with the picture. Write the word.

At Home: Put a card for each of these in a bag: _im, _in, _id, _ad, _an, _am. Take turns picking cards, writing a beginning letter, and reading the word.

Unit 2
Review Blending with Short *i, a*

8

Name _____

I	I	the
and	said	and
said	said	the
is	is	I

Say the first word in the row. Draw a circle around the word where you see it in the same row.

4 Unit 2
Review and, I, is, said

At Home: Have the child practice writing the words *I*, *and*, *is*, and *said* in a tray of salt or sand.

Name _____

Write the letters *Tt*. Say the word that names each picture. Color the picture whose name begins with the same sound as *turtle*.

At Home: Play "Telephone." Whisper a word that begins with *t* in the child's ear. Then the child whispers it to another person, who announces it.

126

Unit 3
Introduce Initial /t/t 8

Name _____

Draw a circle around the airplane that is high. Draw a line under the airplane that is low.
Draw a circle around the animal that is short. Draw a line under the animal that is tall.
Draw a circle around the heavy rock. Draw a line under the object that is light.

At Home: Together compare the heights of things in your home. Which chair is tall? Which is short? Have the child compare weights of toys or cooking utensils by holding one item in each hand.

Unit 3
Introduce Opposites

_t_

Name _____

 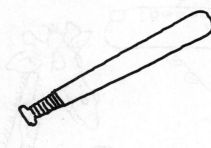 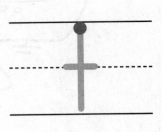

  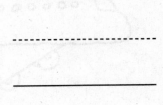

 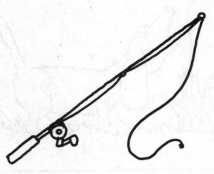

Say the name of each picture. Color the picture whose name has the same ending sound as _hat_. Write the letter _t_.

At Home: Take turns rhyming words that end with _t_, such as _net_, _wet_, _get_, and so on. Repeat with other words that end with _t_ such as _cat_ and _fit_.

Unit 3
Introduce Final /t/t 6

Name _____

Draw a circle around the picture that shows something that could not really happen.

Unit 3
Introduce Fantasy and Reality

At Home: Have the child draw a picture of something that could not happen.

Name _____

Say the name of the picture. Where do you hear the sound /t/*t*? Draw a circle around the first *t* if it is the beginning sound (as in *turtle*). Draw a circle around the second *t* if it is the ending sound (as in *hat*).

At Home: Write *tan*. Together, change the letter *a* to an *i* to make *tin*. Help the child notice that both words begin with *t*.

Unit 3
Review /t/*t*   6

Name _____

🍎

We

and we

   **.**

☆

We

and we

 **.**

Read the sentences by saying the words and telling about the pictures. Draw a line under the word *we* in each sentence.

4 Unit 3
Introduce High-Frequency Words: *we*

At Home: Choose pairs of actions to do together. Take turns saying them aloud: *We ___ and we ___.* Then act out the actions together.

Name _____

N a t

Nat

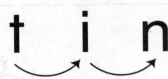

t i n

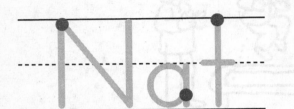

s i t

m a t

Blend the sounds and say the word. Write the word. Draw a line under the picture that goes with the word.

At Home: Make word cards for *tan, tam, Tim, tin, sit,* and *mat.* Take turns reading them and using them in a sentence.

Unit 3
Review Blending with Short a, i

 8

T t

Name _____

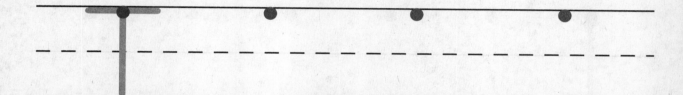

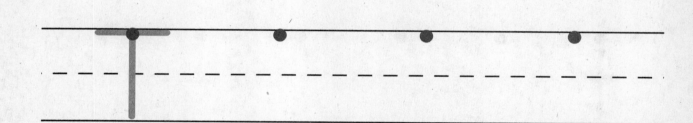

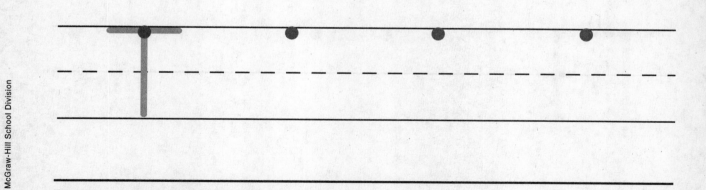

Trace and write capital *T*. Start at the dot.

Unit 3
Handwriting: *T*

At Home: As you practice capital *T*, guide the child to tell what is the same and what is different about writing capital *T* and capital *I*.

Name _____

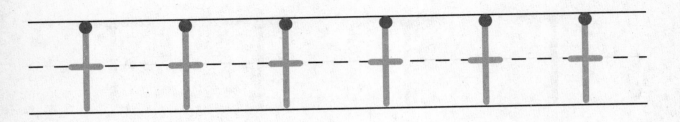

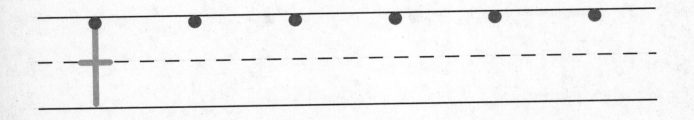

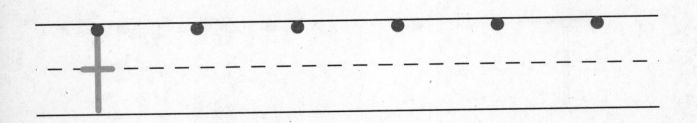

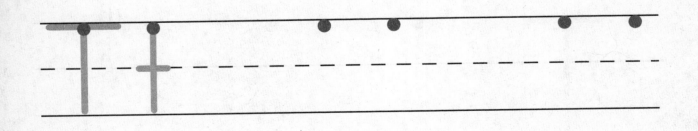

Trace and write lowercase *t*. Start at the dot. On the last line, trace and write *Tt*.

At Home: Practice together making *T* and *t* in sand, dirt, or clay using a stick.

Unit 3
Handwriting: *T, t*
4

134

McGraw-Hill School Division

Name _____

Draw a circle around the picture that shows something that could not really happen.

Unit 3
Review Fantasy and Reality

At Home: Together, read a favorite fantasy story. Have child point out things in the story that could not happen.

Name _____

Tim Tam

Tam

Nat mat

_____

Min Sid

_____

Dad Nan

_____

Look at the picture. Read the words. Draw a line under the word that goes with the picture. Write the word.

At Home: Add these cards to your set: _at and _it. Take turns adding a letter at the left to create words. Use each word in a sentence.

Unit 3
Review Blending with Short *a*, *i*
8

136

Name _____

○ the	we	the
☆ said	said	and
🌲 we	I	we
🐟 the	said	the

Say the word at the beginning of each row. Draw a circle around the word where you see it in the same row.

4   Unit 3
Review we, said, the

At Home: Write the words *we*, *said*, and *the* on separate pieces of paper. Take turns picking words and using them in sentences.

Cc Name _____

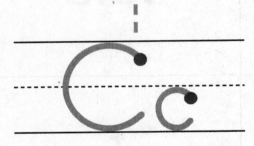

Trace the letters *Cc*. Say the word that names each picture. Color each picture whose name begins with the same sound as *cap*, and draw a line from these pictures to the letters *Cc*.

At Home: Play "Secret Word." Say *I have a secret word that begins with* c *and says meow.* Child gets three guesses. Continue with other words such as *camel, car,* and *cap.*

Unit 3
Introduce Initial /k/c 9

McGraw-Hill School Division

Name _____

Color the tall giraffe yellow. Color the short giraffe orange. Find the bird that is high. Color it blue. Find the bird that is low. Color it red. Draw a line under the heavy elephant. Draw a circle around something that is light.

At Home: Together, point to and say the names of things that are tall and short, high and low, heavy and light.

6 Unit 3
Review Opposites

Cc

Name _____

Write the letters *Cc*. Say the word that names each picture. Color the picture whose name begins with the same sound as *cap*.

McGraw-Hill School Division

At Home: Together, name things whose names begin with *c* and which you can carry in a car: *I can carry a ___ in my car.*

Unit 3
Review Initial /k/c

8

Name _____

🍎

⭐

🌲

Look at the picture on the left. Color the picture on the right that shows what happens next.

Unit 3
Introduce Make Predictions

At Home: Read a story together. After reading each page, ask "What do you think will happen on the next page?" Discuss child's predictions.

Name _____

c

t

Say the picture name. Write the letters that stand for the beginning and ending sounds in each picture name.

At Home: Write *can* and together change it to *cat*. Which letter changed? Which letters stayed the same?

Unit 3
Review /k/c, /t/t

8

142

Name _____

Are we

?

Are we

?

Are we

?

We are

.

Read the sentences. Draw a line under the word *are* in each sentence.

4   Unit 3
Introduce High-Frequency Words: *are*

At Home: Use the word *are* in a question, and then have the child change it to a statement: *Are you ready? You are ready*. Then switch roles.

McGraw-Hill School Division

Name _____

m a n

_____

m a n

c a n

_____

- -

c a t

_____

- -

m a t

_____

- -

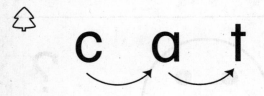

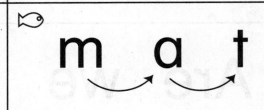

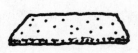

Blend the sounds and say the word. Write the word. Draw a line under the picture that goes with the word.

At Home: Make four cards like this: _a_. Take turns adding beginning and ending letters to make words. Read the words and use them in sentences.

Unit 3
Review Blending with Short *a*

McGraw-Hill School Division

144

Name _____

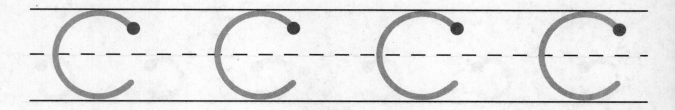

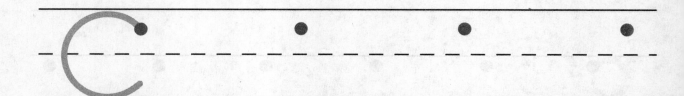

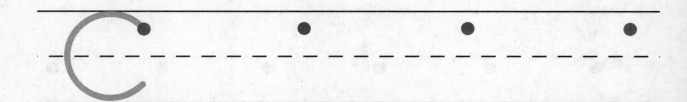

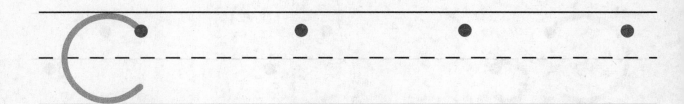

Trace and write capital *C*. Start at the dot.

 **4** Unit 3
Handwriting: *C*

At Home: Together, practice writing *C* by tracing with the index finger on a tabletop.

Cc

Name _____

C C C C C C C C C C C C

C • • • • • •

C • • • • • •

Cc • • • •

Trace and write lowercase *c.* Start at the dot. On the last line, trace and write *Cc.*

At Home: As the child practices *C* and *c,* watch that the lowercase *c* does not rise above the middle of the line space.

McGraw-Hill School Division

Unit 3
Handwriting: *C, c*   4

Name _____

Look at the picture on the left. Color the picture on the right that shows what happens next.

Unit 3
Review Make Predictions

At Home: Play "What Next?" As you do daily tasks, ask the child what you will need to do next after each task is done.

Name _____

sit   tan

sit

Tam   mat

_____

can   cat

_____

tin   Tim

_____

Look at the picture. Read the words. Draw a line under the word that goes with the picture. Write the word.

At Home: Make four cards like this: _i_.Take turns adding
beginning and ending letters to make words.
Read the words and use them in sentences.

Unit 3
Review Blending with Short *a*, *i*

Name _____

⬭	**are**	**are** **we**
☆	**we**	**we** **I**
🌲	**is**	**are** **is**
🐟	**are**	**I** **are**

Say the word at the beginning of each row. Draw a circle around the word where you see it in the same row.

4 Unit 3
Review *are, we, is*

At Home: Take turns using these words in making questions and statements: *We are ___. Are we ___?*

Oo **Name** _____

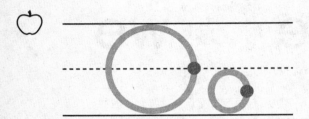  

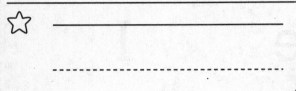  

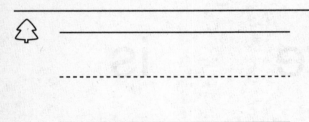  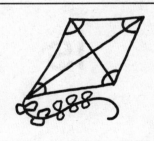

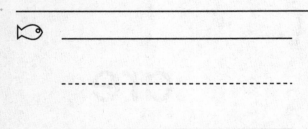  

Write the letters *Oo*. Say the word that names each picture. Color the picture whose name begins with the same sound as *octopus*.

At Home: Make up a story about Ollie Otter and Oliver Octopus. Have the child draw a picture of Ollie and Oliver and help child label each animal.

Unit 3
Introduce Initial /o/o

150

Name _____

Color the items that are *above* the frog. Draw a circle around the items that are *on* the mushroom. Draw a line under the items that are *below* the mushroom. Tell about the things you see in the picture.

13 Unit 3
Introduce Above, On, Below

McGraw-Hill School Division

At Home: Together, look at some shelves in the room. Point out objects that are above, on, or below each other. Have the child identify the position of the objects.

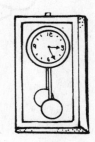

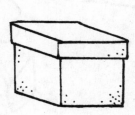

Write the letter *o*. Say the word that names each picture. Color each picture whose name has the same middle sound as *pot*.

At Home: Take turns saying words that rhyme with *cot*.
Write them in a list and note the middle sound and letter.
Do the same for *fox*.

Unit 3
Introduce Medial /o/o
9

McGraw-Hill School Division

152

Name _____

🍎

☆

🌲

Draw a circle around the picture that shows something that could not have really happened.

3 Unit 3
Review Fantasy and Reality

At Home: Take turns changing one part of a familiar activity to make it something that could not really happen: *We ate dinner with a pink dinosaur.*

Name _____

O ⊙   O O   O O

O O   O O   O O

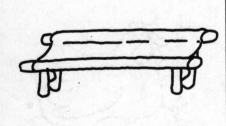

O O   O O   O O

Say the name of the picture. Where do you hear the sound /o/o? Draw a circle around the first o if it is the beginning sound (as in *octopus*). Draw a circle around the second o if it is the middle sound (as in *pot*).

At Home: Find words that rhyme with *cot* (*hot*), *frog* (*log*), and *sock* (*lock*).

Unit 3
Review /o/o   9

Name _____

You can

.

You can

.

You can

.

 ☆ Read the sentence by saying the words and telling about the picture. Draw a circle around the word *you*. ⌂ Read the words. Draw a picture of something a child can do. Then draw a circle around the word *you*.

4 | Unit 3
Introduce High-Frequency Words: *you*

At Home: Play "I Can, You Can." The child says *I can* ___, then you reply *You can* ___. Then act out the actions with the child.

Name _____

⚪🍎 **o n**

on

☆ **M o m**

_____

_____

🌲 **D o t**

_____

_____

🐟 **T o m**

_____

_____

Blend the sounds and say the word. Write the word. Draw a line under the picture that goes with the word.

At Home: Make four cards like this: _ot. Take turns adding *c, n, d,* and *t* to make words. Read the words and use them in sentences.

Unit 3
Introduce Blending with Short *o*

 8

Name _____

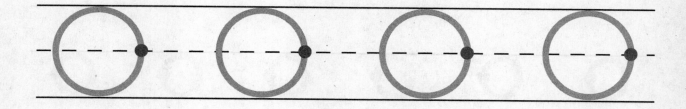

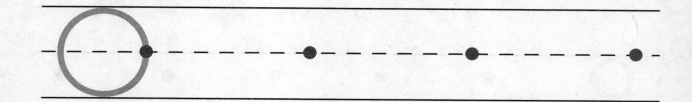

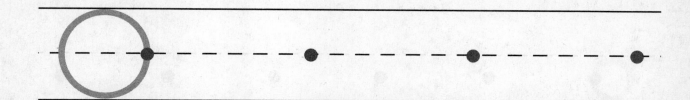

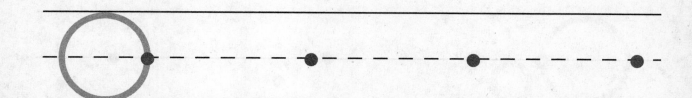

Trace and write capital O. Start at the dot.

 Unit 3
Handwriting: *O*

At Home: Practice making each capital *O* even and smooth as you write together.

Name _____

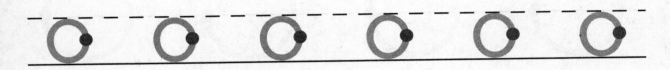

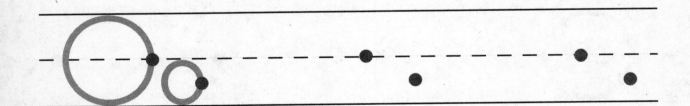

Trace and write lowercase *o*. Start at the dot. On the last line, trace and write *Oo*.

At Home: Practice writing *Oo* as you chant "Oh! Oh! Oh!" together. Encourage the child to form each *O* and *o* with one even circle.

Unit 3
Handwriting: *O, o*

McGraw-Hill School Division

Name _____

Find two things in each picture that could not really happen. Put an X on them.

Unit 3
Review Fantasy and Reality

At Home: Have your child draw a picture that combines fantastic and realistic elements.

Name _____

Mom Dom
dot cot

_____
_____

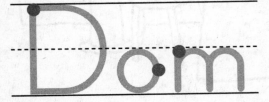

_____
_____

in   on

_____
_____

tan Tim

_____
_____

Look at the picture. Read the words. Draw a line under the word that goes with the picture. Write the word.

At Home: Write *Tim*. Show the child how to change *Tim* to *Tom*. Tell which letter changed. Then have the child change *Tom* to *Tam* and tell what happened to the letter *o*.

Unit 3
Review Blending with Short *o*, *i*

 8

Name _____

🍎 that	that and
⭐ you	you I
🌲 are	and are
🐟 my	my you

Say the word at the beginning of each row. Draw a circle around the word where you see it in the same row.

Unit 3
Review you, are, that, my

At Home: Make up cards for *you, are, that, my*. Ask child to read them to you. Give clues about a word and have the child guess the word you are thinking of—for example, the word rhymes with *cat*.

Ff Name _____

Trace the letters *Ff*. Say the word that names each picture. Color each picture whose name begins with the same sound as *fish*. Draw a line from these pictures to the letters *Ff*.

At Home: Play "I'm Going to Fiji." Take turns naming things you will pack—all of which must begin with *f*.

Unit 3
Introduce Initial /f/f 9

Name _____

Point to the teddy bear on the top shelf. Point to the ship on the middle shelf. Point to the helicopter on the bottom shelf. Draw a ball on the top shelf. Draw a block on the middle shelf. Draw a car on the bottom shelf.

6 Unit 3
Introduce Top, Middle, Bottom

At Home: Choose a bookcase, dresser, or set of shelves. Have the child tell you the contents of the top, middle or bottom drawer or shelf.

Ff   Name _____

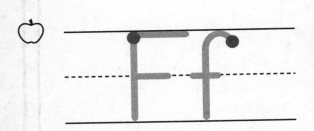  

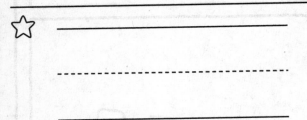  

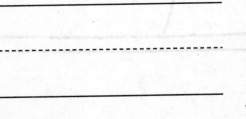  

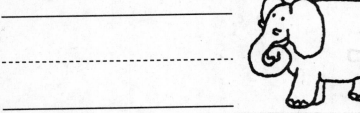  

Write the letters *Ff*. Say the word that names each picture. Color the picture whose name begins with the same sound as *fish*.

At Home: Take turns giving directions to each other such as: face left, face right, face forward. Note the initial *f* in words you use.

Unit 3
Review Initial /f/ f   8

Name _____

🍎

☆

🌲

Look at the picture on the left. Color the picture on the right that shows what happens next.

Unit 3
Review Make Predictions

At Home: Look through pictures in a children's magazine.
Take turns trying to guess what the various articles
will be about.

Ff **Cc**   Name _____

Say the name of each picture. Draw a circle around the letter that stands for the sound you hear at the beginning of each picture name.

McGraw-Hill School Division

At Home: Take turns saying words that begin with the same sounds as *fish* or *cap*. The listener writes the letter for the beginning sound in the air.

Unit 3
Review /f/f, /k/c   6

Name _____

I have a cat.

You have a cat.

You and I have a cat.

Read the sentences. Draw a line under the word *have* in each sentence.

3

Unit 3
Introduce High-Frequency Words: *have*

At Home: Ask the child to draw something he or she has. Have the child write *I have a* over the picture and then read the sentence using the picture name.

Name _____

f a n

f a t

_____

f a n

_____

f i t

f i n

_____

_____

Blend the sounds and say the word. Write the word. Draw a line under the picture that goes with the word.

At Home: Write *in* and *it*. Read the words aloud together. Show the child how to change *in* to the word *if*. Have the child tell you how to change the word *it* to *if*. Take turns using *if* in a sentence.

Unit 3
Review Blending with Short *a*, *i* 8

Ff

Name _____

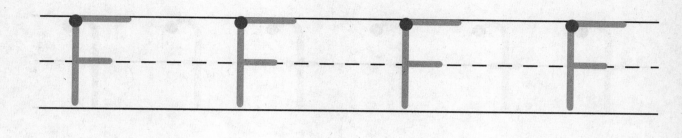

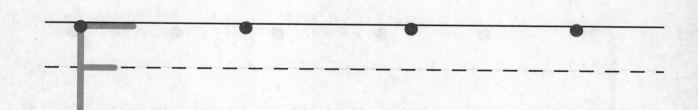

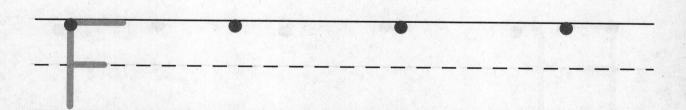

Trace and write capital *F*. Start at the dot.

 Unit 3
Handwriting: *F*

At Home: As your child practices capital *F*, be sure that the top horizontal line is longer than the middle horizontal line.

Ff

Name _____

f f f f f f

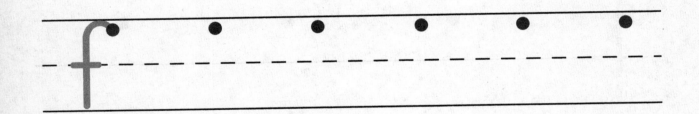

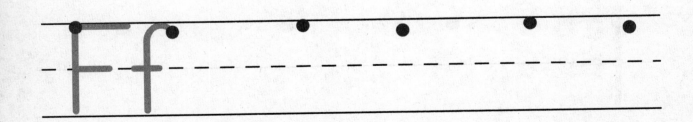

Ff

Trace and write lowercase *f*. Start at the dot. On the last line, trace and write *Ff*.

McGraw-Hill School Division

At Home: As you practice writing lowercase *f*, check to be sure that the child does not have too much trouble with the curve at the top of the letter.

Unit 3
Handwriting: *F, f*
4

Name _____

Look at the picture on the left. Color the picture on the right that shows what happens next.

3 Unit 3
Review Make Predictions

At Home: Look through magazine pictures together. Make two predictions for what could happen next in each situation.

Name _____

sad sit
_____

_____

dot did
_____

_____

fin fan
_____
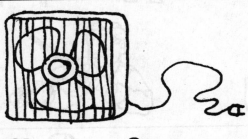
_____

on in
_____
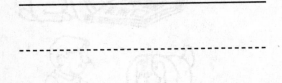
_____

Look at the picture. Read the words. Draw a line under the word that goes with the picture. Write the word.

At Home: Write f_n, f_n. Show the child how to put a after f to make the word *fan*. Have the child show you how to make the word *fin*. Do the same for f_t.

Unit 3

 8

Review Blending with Short a, i, o

McGraw-Hill School Division

Name _____

⏾ We have a cat.
_____

☆ Sam is a tan cat.

🌲 "Is that you, Sam?"
said Dad.

🐟 Sam and Nan are
on the mat.

Read the sentences. Then do the following: ⏾ Draw a circle around the word *have*. Draw a
line under the word *we*. ☆ Draw a circle around the word *is*. 🌲 Draw a circle around the word
you. 🐟 Draw a circle around the word *are*.

5 Unit 3
Review *have, we, you, are, is*

At Home: Make two cards for each word and place the
cards face down on a table. Have the child find the
matching pairs.

Name _____

Look at the letters at the beginning of the row. Color the picture whose name begins with the sound the letters stand for.

At Home: Say the words *turtle*, *cap*, and *fish*. Have the child repeat the word that has the same beginning sound after you say the following words: *tall*, *corn*, *fox*, *fire*, and *camera*.

Unit 3
Review Initial /t/t, /k/c, /f/f

3

Name _____

🍎

⭐

🌲

○ Draw a circle around the object that is heavy. Draw a line under the object that is light. ☆ Draw a circle around the boy who is tall. Draw a line under the boy who is short. ♧ Draw a circle around the objects that are high. Draw a line under the objects that are low. Color the top pictures on the page brown. Color the middle pictures yellow. Color the bottom pictures blue.

9 Unit 3
Review Opposites; Top, Middle, Bottom

At Home: Play "High Low." Take turns saying names of things that are high or low. The listener responds silently by holding a hand up for high and down for low.

_t_ Name _____

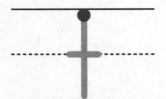 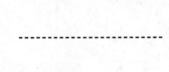 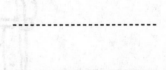

Say the name of each picture. Write the letter _t_ under each picture that has the same ending sound as _hat_.

At Home: Take turns rhyming words with _hat_ and _nut_.
Accept nonsense words but encourage the child to
think of real words.

Unit 3
Review Final /t/t 6

Name _____

Find two things in each picture that could not really happen. Put an X on them.

At Home: Make up a fantasy store. See how many silly or "impossible" products you can think of to sell in your store.

Name _____

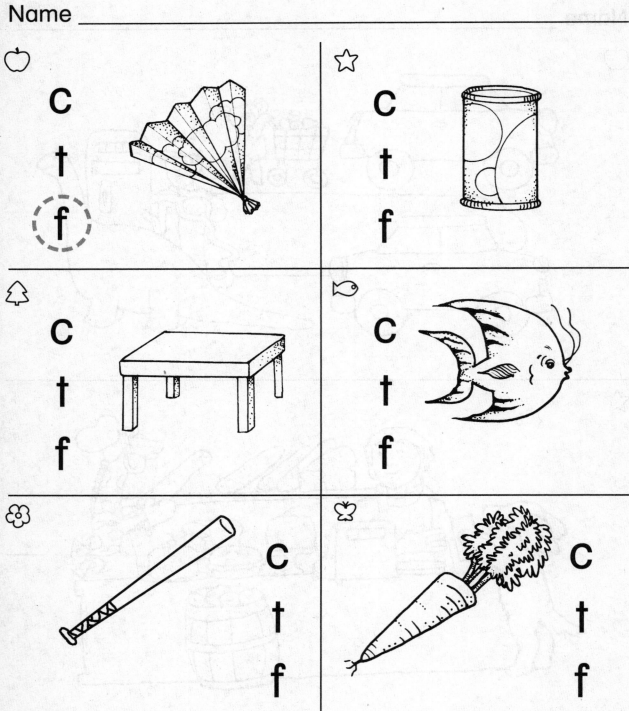

c
t
f

c
t
f

c
t
f

c
t
f

c
t
f

c
t
f

Say the name of each picture. Draw a circle around the letter that stands for the sound you hear at the beginning of each picture name. Say the name of each picture. Draw a circle around the letter that stands for the sound you hear at the end of each picture name.

At Home: Write the word *count*. Say the word together and have the child circle the *c*. Say the word again and have the child underline the *t*.

Unit 3
Review /t/t, /k/c, /f/f

6

McGraw-Hill School Division

Name _____

we	we	my
have	and	have
you	you	my
are	are	have

Say the word at the beginning of each row. Draw a circle around the word where you see it in the same row.

Unit 3
Review we, are, you, have

At Home: Practice making sentences with *we are* and *you are* and with *we have* and *you have*. Have the child draw pictures of things he or she has.

Name _____

 o n

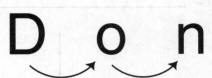 D o n

on

_____

 M o m

 c o t

_____

_____

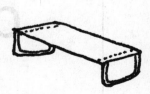 

Blend the sounds and say the word. Write the word. Draw a line under the picture that goes with the word.

At Home: Write *Not I* on two cards. Take turns asking and answering such questions as "Who ate all the cookies?" etc. Hold up a card and say "Not I."

Unit 3
Review Blending with Short *o*

8

Name _____

sad Sid fin

dim dot cot

Trace and write the words.

4 Unit 3
Handwriting Review

At Home: Practice writing other words that
use these letters — for example, *can, cat,
tin, sit, fat.*

Name _____

A cat did it.

Can Tom fit?

Trace and write the sentences.

At Home: As you both write words and sentences, watch to see that good spacing between words is achieved.

Unit 3
Handwriting Review 4

Name _____

Look at the picture on the left. Color the picture on the right that shows what happens next.

Unit 3
Review Make Predictions

At Home: As you perform a task together, predict two actions. See which one turns out to be accurate.

Name _____

sat Sid

sat

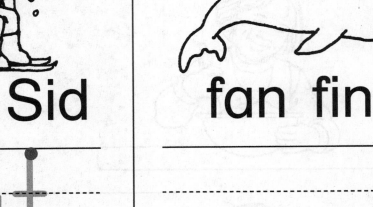

fan fin

_____

Mom Tom

_____

not on

_____

Look at the picture. Read the words. Draw a line under the word that goes with the picture. Write the word.

At Home: Write _a_, _o_, and _i_. Take turns making words with the child by adding letters to either side. Read the words you make and use them in sentences.

184

Unit 3
Review Blending with Short _a_, _i_, _o_ 8

McGraw-Hill School Division

Name _____

We have a tan cat.

☆

You have a tan cat.

🌲

"Are you my cat?" said Tim.

"You are my cat!" said Tim.

Read the sentences. Then do the following: ⭕ Draw a circle around the word *we*. ☆ Draw a circle around the word *have*. 🌲 Draw a circle around the word *you*. 🐟 Draw a circle around the word *are*.

4 Unit 3
Review *we*, *are*, *you*, *have*

At Home: Play a new form of "Go Fish." Make four sets of word cards for the words *we*, *have*, *you*, and *are*. Give three cards to yourself and the child and try to find matches.

Rr Name _____

1.

2.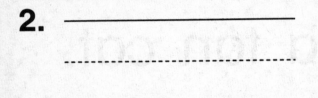

3.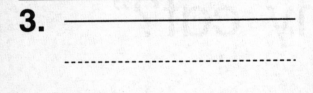

4.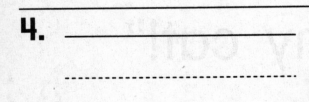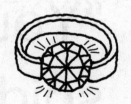

Trace and write the letters *Rr*. Say the word that names each picture. Color the picture whose name begins with the same sound as *rope*.

At Home: Play "I'm Going to Rio Grande." Take turns naming things you will pack. Each thing must begin with *r*.

Unit 4
Introduce Initial /r/r 8

Name _____

Look at the picture. Color the items that are *on* the tree. Draw a circle around the things that are *off* the tree.

Unit 4
Introduce On, Off

At Home: Place common objects on a table and on the floor. Together, talk about the items that are on the table and those that are off.

 Practice 188

Name _____

1.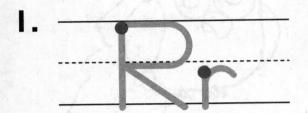

2.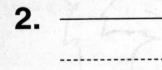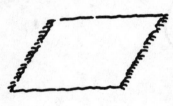

3.

4.

Write the letters *Rr*. Say the word that names each picture. Color the picture whose name begins with the same sound as *rope*.

At Home: Ask the child to name as many color words as possible. Write them down and ask the child to circle the letter *r* wherever it appears.

Unit 4
Review Initial /r/r

8

McGraw-Hill School Division

188

Name _____

I.  ●   ●Sam is sad.

2. ●   ●Min is a cat.

3. ●   ●I ran to Mom.

4. ●   ●Nat is a man.

Look at each picture. Then read the sentences. Draw a line from each picture to the sentence that tells about it.

 Unit 4
Introduce Main Idea

At Home: Say a sentence such as:
Lisa won the race. Have the child draw
a picture to show the idea.

Rr Ff

Name _____

1.

r

f

2.

r

f

3.

r

f

5

4.

r

f

5.

r

f

6.

r

f

Say the name of each picture. Draw a circle around the letter that stands for the sound you hear at the beginning of each picture name.

McGraw-Hill School Division

At Home: Play "Fish in the River." Take turns "catching" something whose name begins with r or f.

Unit 4
Review /r/r, /f/f

6

190

Name _____

1.

Tom ran to the cat.

2.

The cat ran to Nan.

3.

Nan ran to the mat.

4. The cat ran to
the mat.

Read the sentence. Draw a line under the word *to* in the sentence.

Unit 4
Introduce High-Frequency Words: *to*

At Home: Tell about something you need, such as "I need
a snack." The child answers, using the word *to*, such as
"I will go *to* the kitchen."

Name _____

1.

_____

- - - - - - - - - - - - - - - -

ran

_____

2.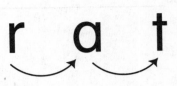

_____

- - - - - - - - - - - - - - - -

_____

3. R o n

_____

- - - - - - - - - - - - - - - -

_____

4. r o d

_____

- - - - - - - - - - - - - - - -

_____

Blend the sounds and say the word. Write the word. Draw a line under the picture that goes with the word.

At Home: Use letter cards to make other words and names using *a, i, o, f, t, c, m, d, s,* and *n.*

Unit 4
Review Blending with Short *a, i, o*

R r

Name _____

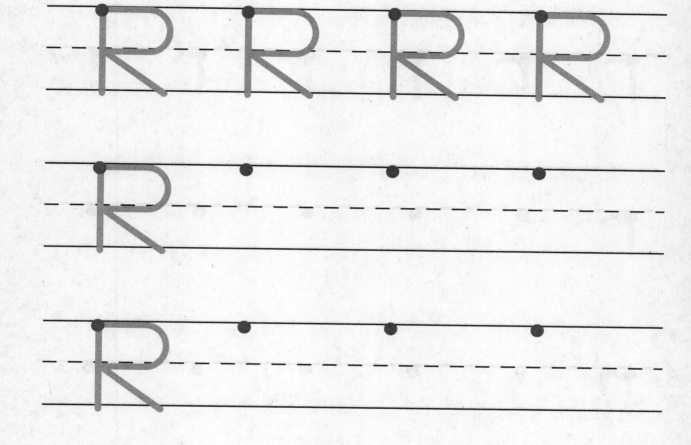

Trace and write capital *R*. Start at the dot.

4 Unit 4
Handwriting: *R*

At Home: As you both write capital *R*, say names such as *Ricky, Ron, Roberto, Rosa,* and so on.

Rr **Name** _____

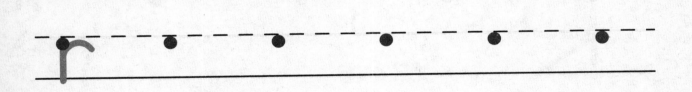

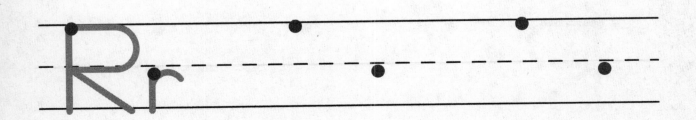

Trace and write lowercase *r*. Start at the dot. On the last line, trace and write *Rr*.

At Home: As you both practice writing *Rr*,
watch for any trouble the child may have
with backtracking the vertical line in *r*.

Unit 4
Handwriting: *R, r*

4

194

Name _____

1.   ● Sid did not fit.

2.  ● ● Ron ran to Tom.

3.  ● ● The cat ran.

4.  ● ● Tam is mad.

Look at each picture. Then read the sentences. Draw a line from each picture to the sentence that tells about it.

Unit 4
Review Main Idea

At Home: Together, pick a picture from a photo album. Have the child say a sentence that tells what the picture is about.

Name _____

1.

in tin

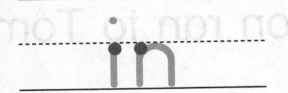
in

2.

man ran

_____

3.

cat rat

4.

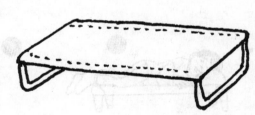

rot cot

Look at the picture. Read the words. Draw a line under the word that goes with the picture.
Write the word.

At Home: Write *did* and show the child how to change
did to *rid*. Have the child tell which letter you changed.
Do the same for *not* to *rot*, *fat* to *rat*, and *can* to *ran*.

Unit 4
Review Blending with Short *a, i, o*

 8

Name _____

1.

"Is the cat on the mat?" said Mom.

2.

The cat ran to Mom.

3.

"Is that my cat?" said Nat.

4.

Nat ran to the cat.

Read the sentences. **1.** Draw a circle around the word *the*. **2.** Draw a circle around the word *to*. **3.** Draw a circle around the word *that*. **4.** Draw a circle around the word *to*. Draw a line under the word *the*.

6 Unit 4
Review *to*, *the*, *that*

At Home: Look for titles of books or movies that contain these words.

Pp Name _____

1.

2.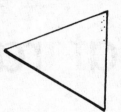

3.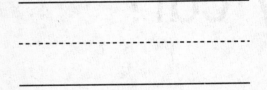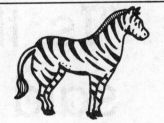

4.

Write the letters *Pp*. Say the word that names each picture. Color the picture whose name begins with the same sound as *pencil*.

McGraw-Hill School Division

At Home: Play "Pop Up." As long as you say words that do not begin with *p*, the child stays down. When you say a word with *p*, the child pops up.

Unit 4
Introduce Initial /p/p

Name _____

1.

2.

3.

Look at the picture on the left. Draw a circle around the picture on the right that shows something you would find inside the building. Draw a line under the picture on the right that shows something you would find outside the building.

 Unit 4
Introduce Inside, Outside

At Home: Take a walk around the block. Have the child choose a building. Take turns naming what might be inside the building. Would it have an elevator? Do people work there?

_p Name _____

Say the name of each picture. Write the letter *p* under each picture that has the same ending sound as *map*.

At Home: Take turns saying the name of something that ends with the sound the letter *p* stands for.

Unit 4
Introduce Final /p/p

6

200

Name _____

Look at the bear on the left. Then look at the pictures below it. Draw a circle around the items found on the bear. Cross out the items that are not on the bear. Do the same thing for the bear on the right. Then use the items to tell how the two bears are the same and different.

 Unit 4
Introduce Compare and Contrast

At Home: Have the child compare his or her clothing with another person's clothing. Help the child see similarities and differences in pants, shirts, shoes and so on.

Name _____

Say the name of each picture. Where do you hear the sound /p/p? Draw a line to the *pencil* if you hear /p/ at the beginning of the word. Draw a line to the *map* if you hear /p/ at the end of the word.

At Home: Look on cereal boxes for words that begin or end with the letter *p*. Say each word. Does *p* begin or end the word?

Unit 4
Review /p/p   6

Name _____

1.

Is Min mad at me?

2.

Is Nat mad at me?

3.

Min and Nat are not mad at me!

Read each sentence. Draw a line under the word *me* in each sentence.

3 Unit 4
Introduce High-Frequency Words: *me*

At Home: Make up rhymes, such as "This is *me* climbing a *tree*." Have the child act out each rhyme.

Name _____

1. P a m

_____

Pam

2. r i p

_____

_____

 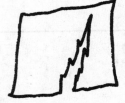

3. t o p

_____

_____

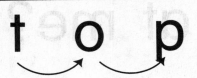 •

4. p i n

_____

_____

 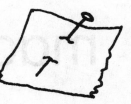

Blend the sounds and say the word. Write the word. Draw a line under the picture that goes with the word.

At Home: Together, write words that begin and end with the same letters. Take turns using some of the words in sentences.

Unit 4
Review Blending with Short *a, i, o*

McGraw-Hill School Division

Name _____

P   P   P   P

P

P

P

Trace and write capital P. Start at the dot.

4 Unit 4
Handwriting: *P*

At Home: As you write capital P, talk together about how capital *P* and capital *F* are alike and how they are different.

McGraw-Hill School Division

P p

Name _____

p p p p p p

p

p

P p

Trace and write lowercase *p*. Start at the dot. On the last line, trace and write *Pp*.

At Home: Take turns saying "*P* is for *Peter*" (or *pickle, Pam,* and so on). If a name is said, write capital *P*. If an object is said, write lowercase *p*.

Unit 4
Handwriting: *P, p*

4

McGraw-Hill School Division

Name _____

Look at the girl on the left. Then look at the pictures below her. Draw a circle around items you see on the girl. Cross out the items that are not on the girl. Do the same thing for the girl on the right. Then use the items to tell how the two girls are the same and different.

Unit 4
Review Compare and Contrast

At Home: Look at a picture in a book together for 5 or 6 seconds but do not discuss what you see. Then shut the book and take turns naming what you saw. Keep a list and check it with the picture.

1.

pin tan

_____

pin

_____

2.

man map

_____

- - - - - - - - - - -

_____

3.

cat cot

_____

- - - - - - - - - - -

_____

4.

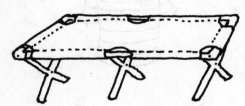

pan nap

_____

- - - - - - - - - - -

_____

Look at the picture. Read the words. Draw a line under the word that goes with the picture. Write the word.

At Home: Together, use letter cards to make the word *cot*. Then change the *o* to *a* to make the word *cat*. Change the vowels in the words *pin* and *tin* to make *pan* and *tan*.

Name _____

I.

| to | to | the |

2.

| me | me | we |

3.

| you | my | you |

4.

| me | my | me |

Read the first word in each row. Draw a circle around the word where you see it in the same row.

McGraw-Hill School Division

At Home: Have the child practice using these words in sentences.

Ll

Name _____

1.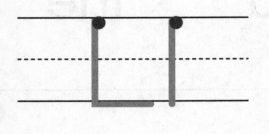

2.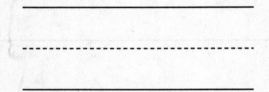

3.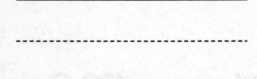

Write the letters *Ll.* Say the word that names each picture. Color the picture whose name begins with the same sound as *lion.*

At Home: Play an *L* game. Give clues such as (lettuce):
What is green, is in a salad, and begins with l?

Unit 4
Introduce Initial /l/ 6

210

Name _____

1.

2.

3.

Color the picture that shows *over*. Draw a line under the picture that shows *under*.

Unit 4
Introduce Over, Under

At Home: Find and talk about items
over or under another item, such
as a chair or a table.

LI

Name _____

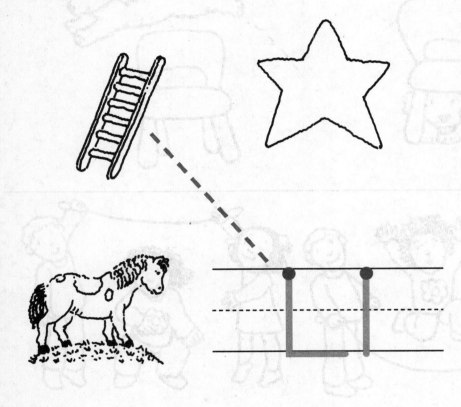

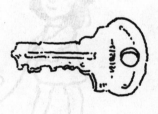

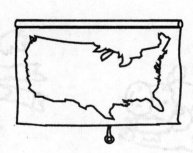

Trace the letters *Ll*. Say the word that names each picture. Color each picture whose name begins with the same sound as *lion*. Draw a line from these pictures to the letters *Ll*.

At Home: If you say a word that begins with *l*, the child "writes" *L* and *l* in the air.

Unit 4
Review Initial /l/
9

Name _____

1.  ● ● Ron is mad.

2.  ● ● I have a dip.

3.  ● ● The lid can fit.

4.  ● ● I have a nap.

Look at each picture. Then read the sentences. Draw a line from each picture to the sentence that tells about it.

Unit 4
Review Main Idea

At Home: Read a story together. Have the child say the main idea of the story: "This story is about ____."

Name _____

1.
l
p

2.
l
p

3.
l
p

4.
l
p

5.
l
p

6.
l
p

1–4. Say the name of each picture. Draw a circle around the letter that stands for the sound you hear at the beginning of each picture name. **5–6.** Say the name of each picture. Draw a circle around the letter that stands for the sound you hear at the end of each picture name.

At Home: Play "Rhyme Time." Say *cap* and ask for words that rhyme. Do the same with *mop, cup, lip.*

Unit 4
Review /l/l, /p/p
6

Name _____

1. "Can we go in?"
said Dan.

2. "We can go in,"
said Mom.

3. "Can the cat go in?"
said Pam.

4. "The cat can go in,"
said Mom.

Read each sentence. Draw a line under the word *go* in each sentence.

Unit 4
Introduce High-Frequency Words: *go*

At Home: Use *go* in questions and
answers, such as *Can I go to the park?*
You can go to the park.

Name _____

1. l i t
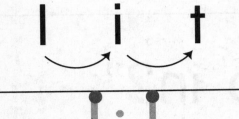

l i t

2. l i p

3. f a n
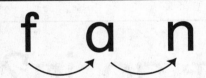

4. r o d

Blend the sounds and say the word. Write the word. Draw a line under the picture that goes with the word.

At Home: Write *not* and *dot*. Have the child change *dot* to *lot* and tell how it was done. Do the same for *dad* to *lad*, *did* to *lid*, and *tap* to *lap*.

Unit 4
Review Blending with Short *a, i, o*

McGraw-Hill School Division

Ll

Name _____

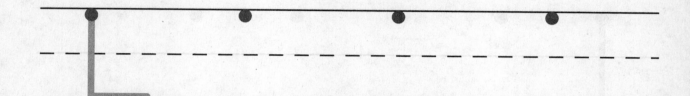

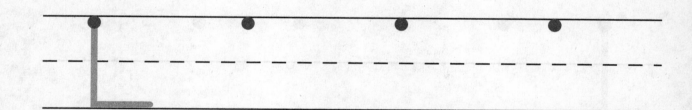

Trace and write capital *L*. Start at the dot.

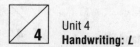

Unit 4
Handwriting: *L*

At Home: As you both practice capital *L*, encourage the child by pointing out how relatively easy this letter is to make.

LI

Name _____

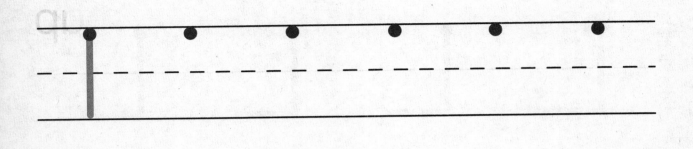

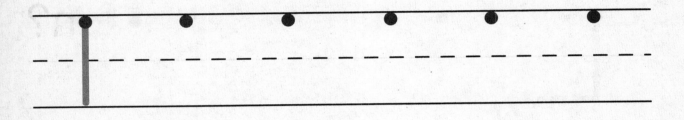

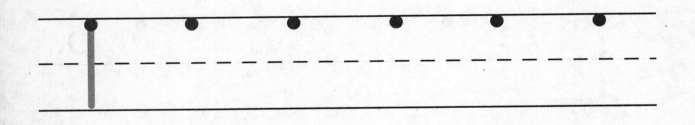

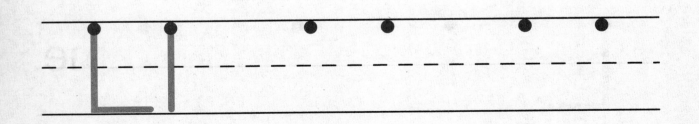

Trace and write lowercase *l*. Start at the dot. On the last line, trace and write *Ll*.

At Home: Together, observe how you can change lowercase *l* to capital *L* in a single stroke.

Unit 4
Handwriting: *L, l* 4

McGraw-Hill School Division

218

Name _____

1.  ● ● I have the map.

2.  ● ● Is that my fan?

3.  ● ● I dip the mop.

4.  ● ● Dom ran to me.

Look at each picture. Then read the sentences. Draw a line from each picture to the sentence that tells about it.

 Unit 4
Review Main Idea

At Home: Watch a commercial on TV together. Take turns saying a sentence to express the main idea of each commercial.

I.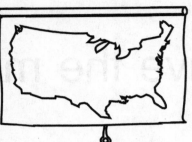

map Pam

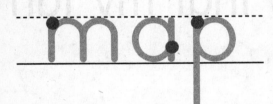

2.

rat Ron

3.

rid lid

4.

Pop Mom

Look at the picture. Read the words. Draw a line under the word that goes with the picture. Write the word.

At Home: Write sound words and read them aloud (*pop*, *tap*, *rap*, *pip*). Take turns making the noises the words describe.

Unit 4 8
Review Blending with Short *a*, *i*, *o*

McGraw-Hill School Division

Name _____

1.		
you	**you**	**my**
2.		
to	**to**	**go**
3.		
me	**my**	**me**
4.		
go	**to**	**go**

Read the first word in the row. Draw a circle around the word where you see it in the same row.

4 Unit 4
Review *go, to, me, you*

At Home: Make several word cards for these words. Mix them up and have the child read and sort them.

Uu

Name _____

I.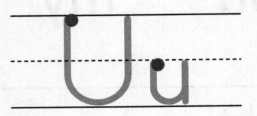

2.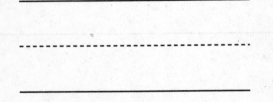

3.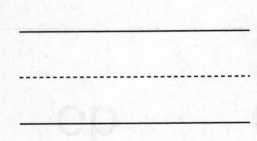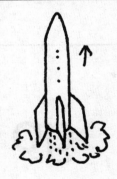

Write the letters *Uu*. Say the word that names each picture. Color the picture whose name begins with the same sound as *umbrella*.

At Home: Play "Jack-in-the-Box." When you say a word that begins with /u/, such as *up*, the child jumps up.

Unit 4
Introduce Initial /u/u

 6

Name _____

Look at the picture. Draw a circle around the things in the picture that are up in the air. Color the things that are down on the ground.

10 Unit 4
Introduce Up, Down

At Home: Name some things that are up (books on shelves, etc.) and some things that are down (rugs, grass, etc.).

_u_

Name _____

- -

u

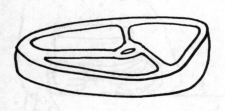  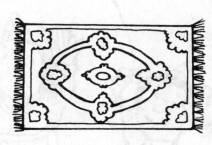

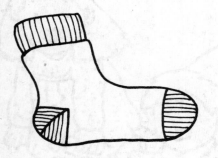  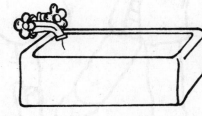

Write the letter _u_. Say the word that names each picture. Listen for the sound in the middle of the word. Color each picture whose name has the same middle sound as _sun_.

At Home: Play "Rhyme Time." Say _sun_ and ask for words that rhyme. Do the same for _nut_ and _rug_.

McGraw-Hill School Division

Name _____

Look at the mat on the left. Then look at the pictures below it. Draw a circle around the items found on the mat. Cross out the items that are not on the mat. Do the same thing for the mat on the right. Then use the items to tell how the two mats are the same and different.

 Unit 4
Review Compare and Contrast

At Home: At dinnertime, compare the plates of food at the table with the child. Then have the child draw a picture of his or her two favorite meals and compare them.

Name _____

 u   u

u   u

u   u

u   u

u   u

u   u

u   u

u   u

u   u

Say the name of the picture. Where do you hear the sound /u/*u*? Draw a circle around the first *u* if it is the beginning sound (as in *umbrella*). Draw a circle around the second *u* if it is the middle sound (as in *sun*).

At Home: Take turns saying words that begin with *under* (*underneath*, *underwater*, and so on). Point out that they begin with the letter *u*.

Unit 4
Review /u/*u*

 9

226

Name _____

1. Do you run in the sun?

2. I do run in the sun.

3. Do you have fun?

4. I do have fun!

Read each sentence. Draw a line under the word *do* in each sentence.

Unit 4
Introduce High-Frequency Words: *do*

At Home: Have the child draw a picture of something he or she does and write *I do* on the picture.

Name _____

1. r u n

_____

run

2. u p

_____

_____

3. p u p

_____

_____

4. s u n

_____

_____

Blend the sounds and say the word. Write the word. Draw a line under the picture that goes with the word.

At Home: Ask the child to write words you say: *up, cup, pup.*
Ask which one names something that can wag its tail.

Unit 4
Introduce Blending with Short *u*

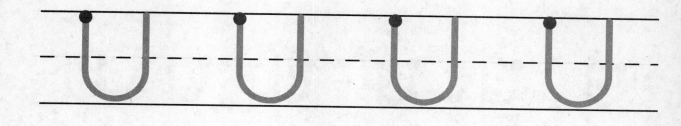

Name _____

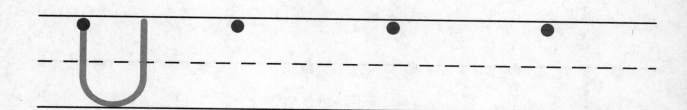

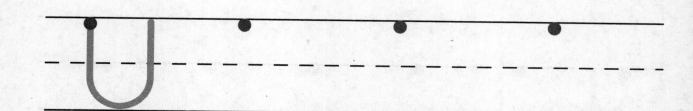

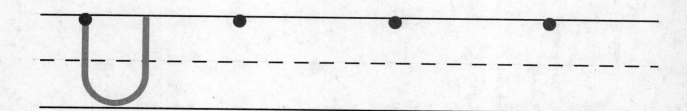

Trace and write capital *U*. Start at the dot.

4 Unit 4
Handwriting: *U*

At Home: Together, practice writing capital *U* in the air.

Uu

Name _____

u u u u u u u

u

u

Uu

Trace and write lowercase u. Start at the dot. On the last line, trace and write Uu.

At Home: Ask the child: Besides their size, what is the difference between capital U and lowercase u? (the vertical stroke in lowercase u)

Unit 4
Handwriting: *U, u*

4

230

McGraw-Hill School Division

Name _____

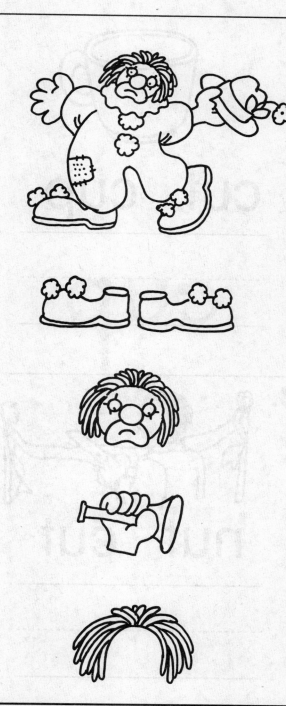

Look at the clown on the left. Then look at the pictures below it. Draw a circle around the items found on the clown. Cross out the items that are not on the clown. Do the same thing for the clown on the right. Tell how the clowns are the same and different.

Unit 4
Review Compare and Contrast

At Home: Have the child draw two clowns that have similarities and differences. Talk about the picture with the child.

Name _____

1.

cut cup

_____

- -

cup

_____

2.

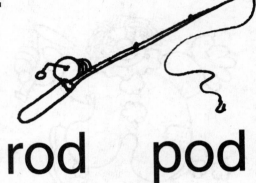

rod pod

_____

- -

_____

3.

nut cut

_____

- -

_____

4.

mop top

_____

- -

_____

Look at the picture. Read the words. Draw a line under the word that goes with the picture.
Write the word.

McGraw-Hill School Division

At Home: Say some of the following words. Have the
child point "up" if the word has the sound that *u* stands
for: *up, cup, fun, pat, sun, mud, bag, pup.*

Unit 4

Review Blending with Short *u, o*

8

Name _____

1. and	said	and
2. go	go	do
3. I	me	I
4. do	to	do
5. me	me	my

Read the first word in each row. Draw a circle around the word where you see it in the same row.

5 Unit 4
Review *do, go, I, and, me*

At Home: Have the child use each of these words in a sentence.

Name _____

1.

Rr

2.

Ll

3.

Pp

Look at the pair of letters at the beginning of each row. Color the pictures whose names begin with the sound the letter stands for.

At Home: Play "What Am I?" Take turns giving clues for words that begin with the letter *r*, *l*, or *p*.

Unit 4
Review Initial /r/r, /p/p, /l/l
6

Name _____

1.

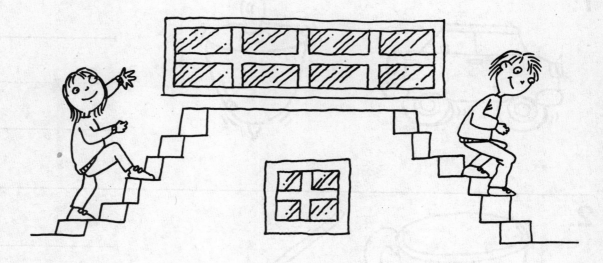

2.

1. Draw a circle around the stairs going *up*. Draw a line under the stairs going *down*. Color the window *over* the stairs blue. Color the window *under* the stairs red. **2.** Draw a circle around the squirrel *on* the roof. Draw a line under the squirrel *off* the roof. Color the bird *inside* the birdhouse red. Color the bird *outside* the birdhouse blue.

Unit 4
Review Positional Terms

At Home: Put a spoon on the kitchen counter. Ask the child to find another spoon that is inside a drawer. Have the child tell which spoon is outside the drawer and which one is inside.

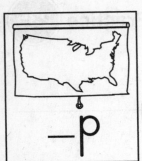

Name _____

1.

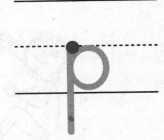

2.

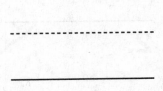

3.

Say the name of each picture. Color the picture whose name has the same ending sound as *map*. Write the letter *p*.

At Home: Have the child add the letter *p* to *cu*, *ca*, *ta*, *ti*, *to*, and then read the words aloud.

Unit 4
Review Final /p/p   6

1.  ●   ●**I run in the mud.**

2. ●   ●**It is fun in the sun.**

3. ●   ●**Pup sat on the mat.**

4. ●   ●**We have a nap.**

Look at each picture. Then read the sentences. Draw a line from each picture to the sentence that tells about it.

Unit 4
Review Main Idea

At Home: Write a sentence such as *I am in the mud*. Have the child draw a picture to show what the sentence is about.

Name _____

1.

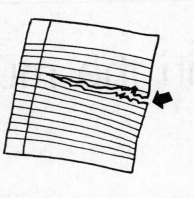

_____ _____

r   p

2.

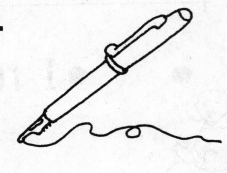

_____ _____

3.

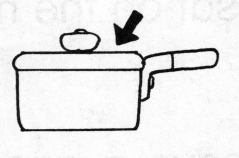

_____ _____

4.

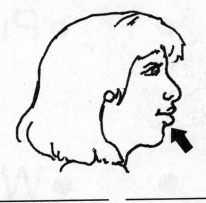

_____ _____

Say the picture name. Write the letters that stand for the beginning and ending sounds in each picture name.

At Home: Make cards with the letters *r*, *p*, and *l* on them.
Say the following words and have the child hold up the
beginning sound: *rat*, *pull*, *leg*, *pear*, *lettuce*, and *robot*.

Unit 4
Review /r/r, /p/p, /l/l

 8

Name _____

1. "Go to Dan!" said Min to the pup.

2. "Do not go in the mud!" said Dad.

3. "Run to me!" said Mom.

4. The pup ran to the mud!

Read the sentences. **1.** Draw a circle around the word *go*. **2.** Draw a circle around the word *do*. **3.** Draw a circle around the word *me*. **4.** Draw a circle around the word *to*.

McGraw-Hill School Division

4 Unit 4
Review *to, me, go, do*

At Home: Make word cards for *go, do, me,* and *to.* Have the child trace and read each card. Mix up the cards and repeat.

Name _____

1. u p

2. c u p

3. n u t

4. m u d

Blend the sounds and say the word. Write the word. Draw a line under the picture that goes with the word.

At Home: Write *up* in the air and blend the sounds as you write. Continue with *mud* and *cup*. Use the words in sentences.

Unit 4
Review Blending with Short *u*

Name _____

lit lip lot

pup ran up

Trace the words. Then write the words.

4 Unit 4
Handwriting Review

At Home: Together, say and write other words that use
these letters (for example, *map*, *rip*).

McGraw-Hill School Division

Name _____

Run to Pat.

Mud is fun!

Trace the words in the sentence. Then write the words.

McGraw-Hill School Division

At Home: Make sure that the child is holding his/her pencil
comfortably and correctly.

Unit 4
Handwriting Review 4

Name _____

Look at the robot on the left. Then look at the pictures below it. Draw a circle around the items found on the robot. Cross out the items that are not on the robot. Do the same thing for the robot on the right. Then use the items to tell how the two robots are the same and different.

Unit 4
Review Compare and Contrast

At Home: Take a walk outside and look at two items (trees, cars, houses). Have the child tell what is the same and different about each item.

McGraw-Hill School Division

Name _____

1.

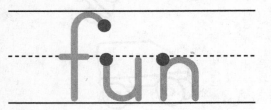

fun fin

_____

fun

2.

Mom mop

_____

- - - - - - - - - - - - - -

_____

3.

rut run

_____

- - - - - - - - - - - - - -

_____

4.

top tip

_____

- - - - - - - - - - - - - -

_____

Look at the picture. Read the words. Draw a line under the word that goes with the picture. Write the word.

At Home: Write *fin*. Ask the child to change *fin* to *fun*.
Take turns. Change *fun* to *run* and change *fun* to *sun*.

Unit 4
Review Blending with Short *u, o, i*   8

Name _____

1.

go   do   to

2.

we   me   my

3.

to   go   do

4.

go   the   is

1. Draw a circle around the word *to*. 2. Draw a line under the word *me*. 3. Draw a circle around the word *do*. 4. Draw a line under the word *go*.

4 Unit 4
Review *to*, *me*, *go*, *do*

At Home: Write the words *to*, *me*, *go*, and *do* on a sheet of paper. Have the child read the words and name the words that rhyme (*to*, *do*).

Kk

Name _____

1.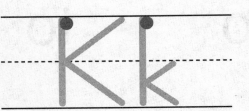

2.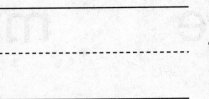

3.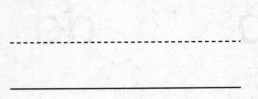

4.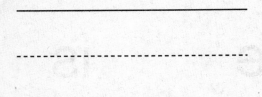

Write the letters *Kk*. Say the word that names each picture. Color the picture whose name begins with the same sound as *kite*.

At Home: Take turns thinking of names for people or pets that begin with *K*. Make a list of them and have the child write *K* at the top of the list.

246

Unit 5
Introduce Initial /k/k   8

Name _____

1.

2.

3.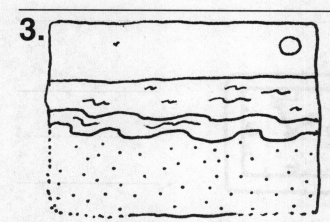

Look at the pictures in each row. Draw a circle around the person in each row. Color the place in each row. Draw a line under the thing in each row.

 Unit 5
Introduce Naming Words

At Home: Have the child draw a picture of a favorite place to visit. Ask the child to point to the people and things in the picture. Then discuss the place.

McGraw-Hill School Division

_ck

Name _____

1.

ck

2.

3.

Say the name of each picture. Color the picture whose name has the same ending sound as *lock*. Write the letters *ck*.

At Home: Talk about and write "sound" words that end with *ck*. You say the words and the child repeats them: *click, tick tock, clickety clack, yackity yack.*

Unit 5
Introduce Final /k/ck 6

Name _____

1.

3 _____ 1 _____ 2 _____

2.

_____ _____ _____

3.

_____ _____ _____

Look at the pictures. Write *1* on the line under the picture that shows the beginning of the story. Write *2* on the line that shows the middle of the story. Write *3* on the line that shows the end of the story.

 Unit 5
Introduce Story Structure

At Home: Read a story with the child. Afterwards, have the child tell what happened in the beginning, middle, and end of the story.

Kk | _ck Name _____

1.

(k) ck

2.

k ck

3.

k ck

4.

k ck

5.

k ck

6.

k ck

Say the name of the picture. Where do you hear the sound /k/k or /k/ck ? Draw a circle around the first k if it is the beginning sound (as in *kite*). Draw a circle around *ck* if it is the ending sound (as in *lock*).

At Home: Play "Mystery Word." Take turns giving clues for words that begin or end with /k/—for example, *I'm thinking of a word that is an animal that has a pouch and jumps (kangaroo).*

Unit 5
Review /k/k, /k/ck   6

250

Name _____

1. "Is the cap for me?" said Tom.

2. "The cap is for you," said Kim.

3. "Is the pup for me?" said Pam.

4. "The pup is for you," said Mom.

Read the sentence. Draw a line under the word *for* in the sentence.

4 Unit 5
Introduce High-Frequency Words: *for*

At Home: Help the child find the word *for* in a magazine or newspaper article.

Name _____

1. n a p

nap

2. d u ck

3. s o ck

4. T i m

Blend the sounds and say the word. Write the word. Draw a line under the picture that goes with the word.

At Home: Give a set of clues: "It begins with s. It ends with ck. It has a short o in the middle. Name that word!" Continue with other words.

Unit 5
Review Blending with Short a, i, o, u

8

McGraw-Hill School Division

Name _____

K K K K

K

K

K

Trace and write capital *K*. Start at the dot.

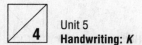

Unit 5
Handwriting: *K*

At Home: Take turns saying names of people and places beginning with *K*—for example, *Katie*, *Kansas*, *Kim*, and *Kenya*. Both of you write capital *K* for each name.

Kk

Name _____

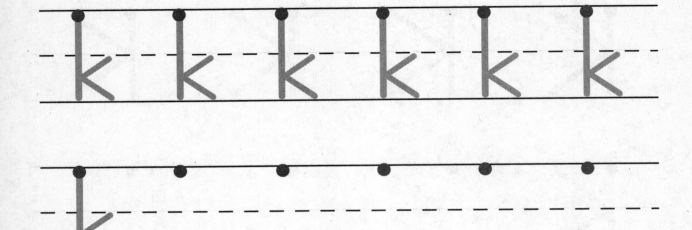

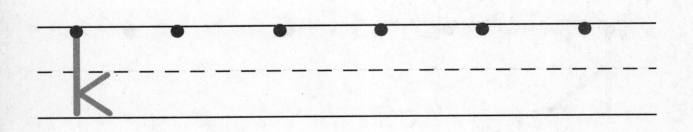

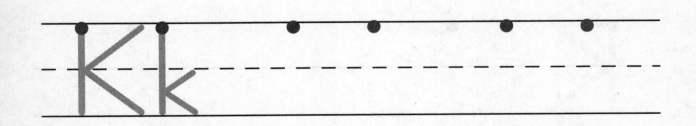

Trace and write lowercase k. Start at the dot. On the last line, trace and write Kk.

At Home: As you practice, guide the child to see that the side strokes in lowercase k are half the length of those in capital K.

Unit 5
Handwriting: K, k

Name _____

I.

3   I   2

_____   _____   _____

2.

_____   _____   _____

3.

_____   _____   _____

Look at the pictures. Write *1* on the line under the picture that shows the beginning of the story. Write *2* on the line that shows the middle of the story. Write *3* on the line that shows the end of the story.

Unit 5
Review Story Structure

At Home: One morning, talk about the beginning, middle, and ending steps of getting dressed in the morning.

Name _____

1.

pup cup
_____

pup

2.

man Nan
_____
_____

3.

Tom tip
_____
_____

4.

lit lock
_____
_____

Look at the picture. Read the words. Draw a line under the word that goes with the picture. Write the word.

At Home: Write *l_ck*. have the child supply the missing letter (*i*, *u*, or *o*) and read the word. Use it in a sentence. Continue with *s_ck* (*i*, *u*, *o*, or *a*) and *t_ck* (*i*, *u*, *o*, or *a*).

Unit 5 8
Review Blending with Short *a*, *i*, *o*, *u*

McGraw-Hill School Division

Name _____

1.

I have a cap for you.

2.

I have a cap for me.

3.

I have a cap for Dad.

4.

I have a cap for Mom.

Read each sentence. **1.** Draw a circle around the word *for*. Draw a line under the word *you*. **2.** Draw a circle around the word *for*. Draw a line under the word *me*. **3–4.** Draw a circle around the word *for*.

McGraw-Hill School Division

6 Unit 5
Review *for, you, me*

At Home: Both of you draw pictures as gifts. Write *for you* on the pictures and exchange them.

Gg

Name _____

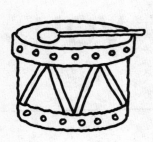

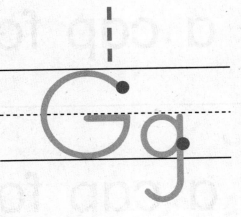

Gg

Trace the letters *Gg*. Say the word that names each picture. Color each picture whose name begins with the same sound as *gift*. Draw a line from these pictures to the letters *Gg*.

At Home: Play "I'm Going to Go to Galveston." Take turns naming things you will pack whose names begin with *g*.

Unit 5
Introduce Initial /g/g

9

258

Name _____

1.

2.

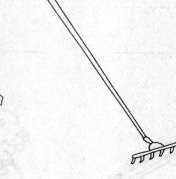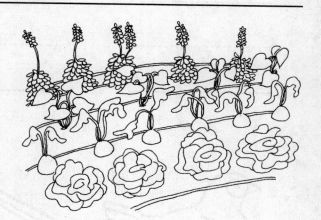

3.

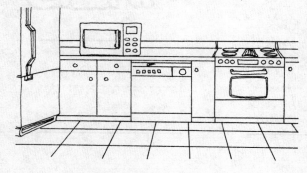

Look at the pictures in each row. Draw a circle around the *person*. Color the *place*. Draw a line under the *thing*.

 Unit 5
Review Naming Words

At Home: Together, page through a magazine. Look for three categories of naming words (i.e., animals, people, and things).

_g

Name _____

_____

_____

_____

g

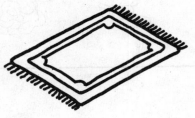

_____

_____

_____

Say the name of each picture. Write the letter *g* under each picture that has the same ending sound as *frog*.

At Home: Take a walk to find words that end with *g*. Look at street signs, store windows, everywhere. *Jog* when you find one.

Unit 5
Introduce Final /g/g

6

Name _____

1.

2.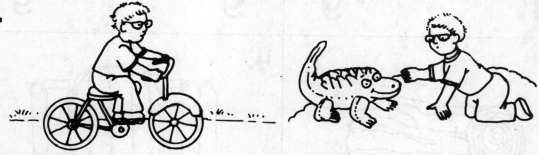

3.

4.

Look at the pictures in each row. Draw a circle around the picture that shows something that happened in "Any Kind of Dog." Then use the pictures you circled to retell the story.

Unit 5
Introduce Summarize

At Home: Take turns with the child in telling family members about a story he or she likes.

Name _____

1.

(g)　　　　　g

2.

g　　　　　g

3.

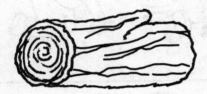

g　　　　　g

4.

g　　　　　g

5.

g　　　　　g

6.

g　　　　　g

Say the name of the picture. Where do you hear the sound /g/ *g*? Draw a circle around the first *g* if it is the beginning sound (as in *gift*). Draw a circle around the second *g* if it is the ending sound (as in *frog*).

At Home: Have the child say "good" every time you say a word that begins with the same sound as *gift*.

Unit 5
Review /g/ *g*

Name _____

1.

"I am IT," he said.

2.

He ran and ran.

3.

Can he tap Sid?

4.

He did!

Read each sentence. Draw a circle around the word *he* in each sentence.

Unit 5
Introduce High-Frequency Words: *he*

At Home: Together, look at pictures in a magazine. Have the child point out a man or boy and say what *he* is doing.

Name _____

1.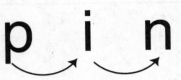

---

pin

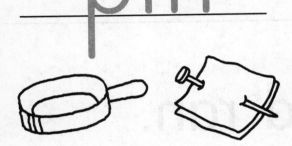

2.

- - - - - - - - - - - - - - -

3. l o g

- - - - - - - - - - - - - - -

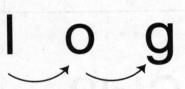

4. r a g

- - - - - - - - - - - - - - -

Blend the sounds and say the word. Write the word. Draw a line under the picture that goes with the word.

McGraw-Hill School Division

At Home: Write a word that rhymes with one of the words the child wrote and say it. Have the child underline the rhyming word with a finger.

Unit 5
Review Blending with
Short *a, i, o, u*

 8

Gg

Name _____

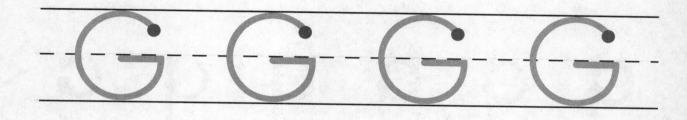

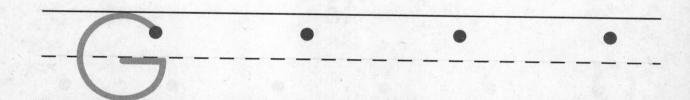

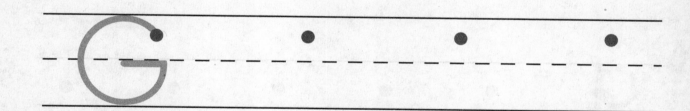

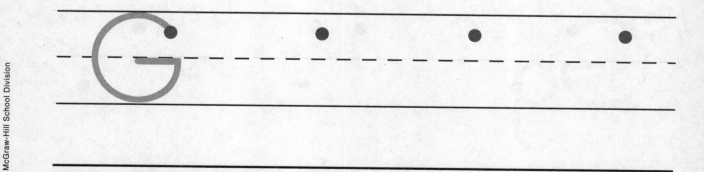

Trace and write capital G. Start at the dot.

Unit 5
Handwriting: G

At Home: Together, practice writing capital G in the air.

Gg

Name _____

g g g g g g

g • • • • •

g • • • • •

Gg • •

• •

Trace and write lowercase *g*. Start at the dot. On the last line, trace and write *Gg*.

At Home: As you both practice lowercase *g*, guide the child to see that it is made like lowercase *a*, but with a "tail."

Unit 5
Handwriting: G, g

Name _____

1.

2.

3.

4.

McGraw-Hill School Division

Look at the pictures in each row. Draw a circle around the picture that shows something that happened in "Pug." Then use the pictures you circled to retell the story.

4 Unit 5
Review Summarize

At Home: Take turns retelling a favorite story without looking at the book.

Name _____

1.

mug man

2.

sock sick

_____

3.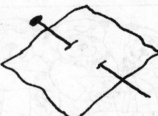

pin pick

4.

rack run

Look at the picture. Read the words. Draw a line under the word that goes with the picture. Write the word.

At Home: Take turns finding words in newspaper headlines that the child can read. Underline them and read them aloud together.

Unit 5
Review Blending
with Short *a, i, o, u*

8

Name _____

1.

we   he   to

2.

are   have   for

3.

is   it   in

4.

me   the   he

1. Draw a circle around the word *he*. 2. Draw a circle around the word *for*.
3. Draw a circle around the word *is*. 4. Draw a circle around the word *he*.

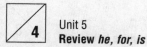

4 Unit 5
Review *he, for, is*

At Home: Ask the child to make up three questions, each
using one of these words.

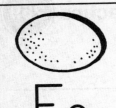

E e Name _____

1.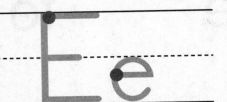

2.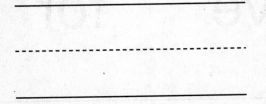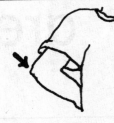

3.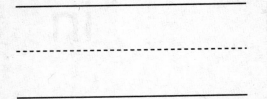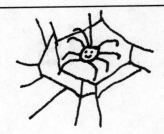

4.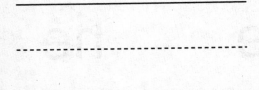

Write the letters *Ee*. Say the word that names each picture. Color the picture whose name begins with the same sound as *egg*.

At Home: Take turns making up sentences using words that begin with /e/e: *Ed bought excellent eggs from Edna. Emma examined the elephant.*

Unit 5
Introduce Initial /e/e

Name _____

1.

the   sit   man

2.

Tim   ran   cat

3.

cut   fin   and

4.

you   we   pat

Circle the word that describes an action.

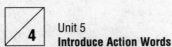

Unit 5
Introduce Action Words

At Home: Have the child name three action words and act them out.

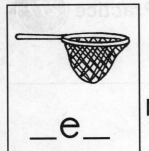

__e__   Name _____

e e

Write the letter *e*. Say the word that names each picture. Listen for the sound in the middle of the word. Color each picture whose name has the same middle sound as *net*.

At Home: Take turns saying other words that have the /e/ sound as in *red*, *peg*, *set*, and so on. Help the child find at least two of these words that rhyme (for example, *bed/red*).

Unit 5
Introduce Medial /e/e / 9

Name _____

1.

3 _____   2 _____   1 _____

2.

_____   _____   _____

3.

_____   _____   _____

Look at the pictures. Write *1* on the line under the picture that shows the beginning of the story. Write *2* on the line that shows the middle of the story. Write *3* on the line that shows the end of the story.

 9 Unit 5
Review Story Structure

At Home: Ask about the child's day at school. Fold a piece of paper into three sections. Have the child draw what happened in the beginning, the middle, and the end of the day.

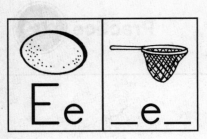 Name _____

e e

e e

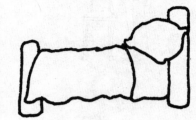

e e

e e

e e

e e

e e

e e

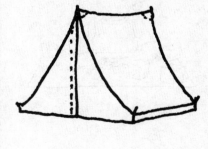

e e

Say the name of the picture. Where do you hear the sound /e/e? Draw a circle around the first *e* if it is the beginning sound (as in *egg*). Draw a circle around the second *e* if it is the middle sound (as in *net*).

At Home: Find things that have initial /e/e (*egg*) or medial /e/e (*vest*) in them.

Unit 5
Review /e/e

9

Name _____

1.

Can she run?

2.

She can run!

3.

She is a lot of fun!

4.

She is my cat, Dot.

Read each sentence. Then draw a line under the word *she* in each sentence.

Unit 5
Introduce High-Frequency Words: *she*

At Home: Look through a magazine together. Have the child
find a picture of a girl or woman and say what *she* is doing.

Name _____

1. n e t

net

2. t e n

10 9

3. p e n

4. m e n

Blend the sounds and say the word. Write the word. Draw a line under the picture that goes with the word.

McGraw-Hill School Division

At Home: Write *p_n* three times. Have the child make words by adding *a*, *i*, and *e* on the blanks. Say each word and use it in a sentence.

276

Unit 5
Introduce Blending with Short *e*

8

Ee

Name _____

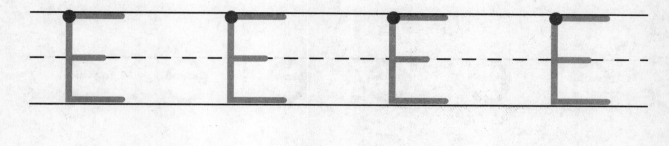

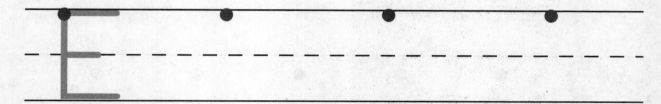

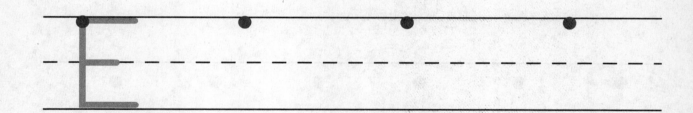

Trace and write capital *E*. Start at the dot.

Unit 5
Handwriting: *E*

At Home: Ask the child: What is the difference between capital *E* and capital *F*? (*E* has a horizontal line at its bottom.)

Ee

Name _____

e e e e e e

e ● ● ● ● ●

e ● ● ● ● ●

Ee ● ● ●
    ● ● ●

Trace and write lowercase *e*. Start at the dot. On the last line, trace and write *Ee*.

At Home: Together, practice writing *Ee*. As you write, talk about how the two forms of the letter are the same and how they are different.

Unit 5
Handwriting: *E, e*

4

278

Name _____

1.

2   1   3

_____   _____   _____

2.

_____   _____   _____

3.

_____   _____   _____

Look at the pictures. Write *1* on the line under the picture that shows the beginning of the story. Write *2* on the line that shows the middle of the story. Write *3* on the line that shows the end of the story.

Unit 5
Review Story Structure

At Home: Take turns telling the beginning, middle, and end of each other's favorite stories.

1.

leg   let

leg

2.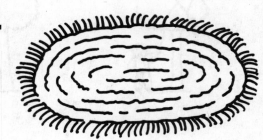

rug   red

3.

pet   pen

4.

fin   fed

Look at the picture. Read the words. Draw a line under the word that goes with the picture. Write the word.

At Home: Take turns rhyming words with these short *e* and short *u* words: *red, leg, let, mug, fun, up.*

Unit 5

Review Blending with Short *e*, *u*

Name _____

1. He got a pup
for Kim.

2. She got a tag for
the pup.

3.

The pup is tan.

4.

The tag is red.

Read each sentence. **1.** Draw a circle around the word *he*. Draw a line under the word *for*.
2. Draw a circle around the word *she*. Draw a line under the word *for*. **3–4.** Draw a circle
around the word *is*.

6 Unit 5
Review she, he, for, is

At Home: Take turns finding *he*, *she*, *for*, and *is* in a
newspaper. Which one occurs most often?

McGraw-Hill School Division

Name _____

Trace the letters *Bb*. Say the word that names each picture. Color each picture whose name begins with the same sound as *book*. Draw a line from these pictures to the letters *Bb*.

At Home: Together, look for things at home whose names begin with /b/*b*. Have the child shout "Boo!" whenever a /b/ word is found.

Unit 5
Introduce Initial /b/*b*

Name _____

1.

pick   he   that

2.

dip   Mom   I

3.

my   sip   man

4.

pup   tin   go

Circle the word that describes an action.

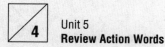
Unit 5
Review Action Words

At Home: Have a glass of juice together. Ask the child to *sip* his or her drink.

_b Name _____

1.

  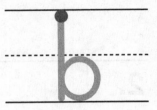

2.

3.

Say the names of the pictures in each row. Color the picture whose name has the same ending sound as *tub*. Write the letter *b*.

At Home: Together, find other words that end with /b/*b*.
Write some of the words in a list and ask the child to draw a
circle around the final letter *b* in each word.

Unit 5
Introduce Final /b/*b*
6

Name _____

1.

2.

3.

4.

Look at the pictures in each row. Draw a circle around the picture that shows something that happened in "The Enormous Carrot." Then use the pictures you circled to retell the story.

Unit 5
Review Summarize

At Home: Take turns telling each other what a favorite movie was about.

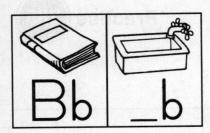

_b Name _____

1.

ⓑ   b

2.
b      b

3.

b   b

4.
b   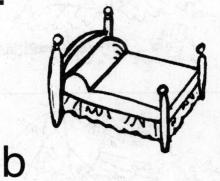   b

5.
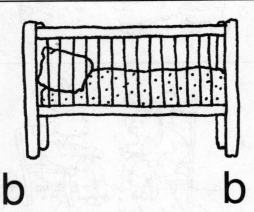
b   b

6.
b   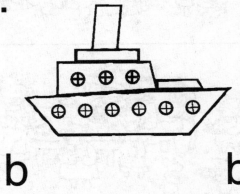   b

Say the name of each picture. Where do you hear the sound /b/b? Draw a circle around the first *b* if it is the beginning sound (as in *book*). Draw a circle around the second *b* if it is the ending sound (as in *tub*).

At Home: What do the words *bib* and *Bob* have in common?
(They start and end with /b/b.) Discuss together. Can you
think of other words like these?

Unit 5
Review /b/b   6

Name _____

1. Kim has a bug
in a bag.

2. Ben has a duck
in a pen.

3. Min has a cat
on the bed.

4. Ron has a bug,
a duck, and a cat!

Read the sentence. Then draw a line under the word *has*.

4 Unit 5
Introduce High-Frequency Words: *has*

At Home: Use *has* in a sentence such as: "A monkey has a tail." If the sentence is true, have the child spell the word *has* in the air. Repeat with other sentences.

Name _____

1. b u g

bug

2. b e d

3. t u b

4. d i g

Blend the sounds and say the word. Write the word. Draw a line under the picture that goes with the word.

At Home: Put *a, e, i, o,* and *u* on pieces of paper. Take turns choosing a letter and making a word by writing a letter on each side of it. Use the word in a sentence.

Unit 5
Review Blending with Short *a, e, i, o, u*

 8

Name _____

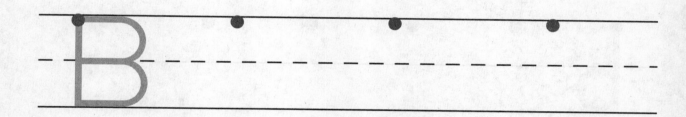

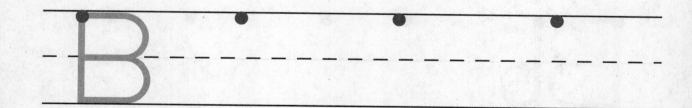

Trace and write capital *B*. Start at the dot.

Unit 5
Handwriting: *B*

At Home: Say aloud to the child a variety of names for
persons and places. When you say a name that begins
with *B*, the child writes capital *B*.

Bb

Name _____

b b b b b b

b

b

Bb

Trace and write lowercase *b*. Start at the dot. On the last line, trace and write *Bb*.

At Home: As you both practice writing *Bb*, watch that the child does not confuse lowercase *b* with lowercase *d*.

McGraw-Hill School Division

Unit 5
Handwriting: *B, b* 4

290

Name _____

1.

2.

3.

4.

Look at the pictures in each row. Draw a circle around the picture that shows something that happened in "A Big Bug." Then use the pictures you circled to retell the story.

4 Unit 5
Review Summarize

At Home: Take turns retelling a favorite fairy tale or folk tale.

Name _____

1.

rub cub

_____

~~cub~~

_____

2.

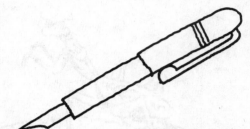

pen ten

_____

- - - - - - - - - - - - - - -

_____

3.

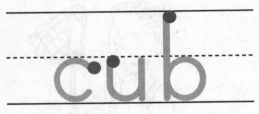

but bat

_____

- - - - - - - - - - - - - - -

_____

4.

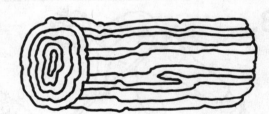

log fog

_____

- - - - - - - - - - - - - - -

_____

Look at the picture. Read the words. Draw a line under the word that goes with the picture.
Write the word.

At Home: Write *p_g*. Take turns adding *a, e, i, o,* and *u.* If
you decide the word you've made is a real word, circle it.
Continue with *b_t.*

Unit 5
Review Blending with Short *a, e, i, o, u*

8

Name _____

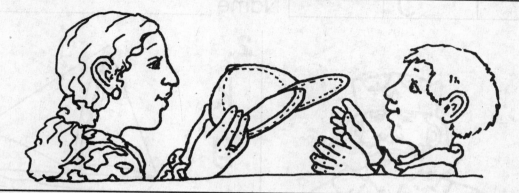

1. "Is it for me?"
he said.

2. "It is for you,"
she said.

3. Mom has a cap
for me!

Read each sentence. **1.** Draw a line under the words *me* and *he*. **2.** Draw a line under the words *for* and *she*. **3.** Draw a line under the word *has*.

Unit 5
Review *has*, *he*, *she*, *me*, *for*

At Home: Make letter cards for the letters *a, e, f, h, m, o, r,* and *s.* Have the child make the words *has, he, she, me,* and *for.*

Kk Gg Bb

Name _____

1.
k
g
b

2.
k
g
b

3.
k
g
b

4.
k
g
b

5.
k
g
b

6.
k
g
b

Say the name of each picture. Draw a circle around the letter that stands for the sound you hear at the beginning of each picture name.

At Home: Make k, g, and b letter cards. Show them one at a time. Have the child say a word that starts with the selected letter.

Unit 5
Review Initial /k/k, /g/g, /b/b
6

Name _____

1.

mad   Kim   hop

2.

kick   Sid   my

3.

Sam   for   dig

4.

pack   the   cat

Draw a circle around the word that describes an action. Draw a line under the word that names a person, place, or thing.

8 Unit 5
Review Naming and Action Words

At Home: Take turns making real or funny sentences using some of the words on this page.

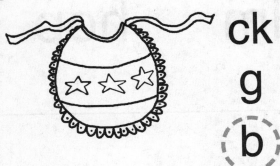 _ck	_g	_b

Name _____

1.
ck
g
(b)

2.
ck
g
b

3.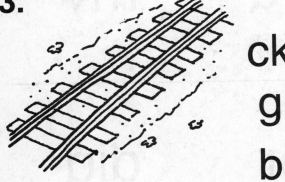
ck
g
b

4.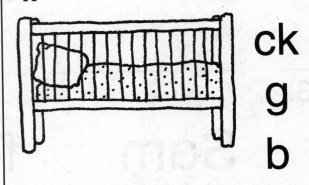
ck
g
b

5.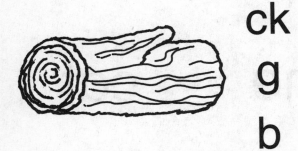
ck
g
b

6.
ck
g
b

Say the name of each picture. Draw a circle around the letter or letters that stand for the sound you hear at the end of each picture name.

McGraw-Hill School Division

At Home: Together, name objects whose names end with these sounds (*mug, lock, cab,* and so on). Help the child listen for any words that rhyme (for example, *clock/lock*).

Unit 5
Review Final /k/ck, /g/g, /b/b   6

Name _____

1.

3   1   2

_____   _____   _____

2.

_____   _____   _____

3.

_____   _____   _____

Look at the pictures. Write *1* on the line under the picture that shows the beginning of the story. Write *2* on the line that shows the middle of the story. Write *3* on the line that shows the end of the story.

Unit 5
Review Story Structure

At Home: After a familiar activity, briefly review the first part, middle part, and last part and then number them 1, 2, 3. For example: 1. Cook supper. 2. Eat supper. 3. Do the dishes.

Name _____

1.

k
(g)
b

2.

k
g
b

3.

k
g
b

4.

ck
g
b

5.

ck
g
b

6.

ck
g
b

1–3. Say the name of each picture. Draw a circle around the letter that stands for the sound you hear at the beginning of each picture name. **4–6.** Say the name of each picture. Draw a circle around the letter or letters that stand for the sound you hear at the end of each picture name.

At Home: Together, find words that combine any two of these sounds: *k, g, b*—for example, *bug, kick, back*.

Unit 5
Review /k/k, /k/ck, /g/g, /b/b

6

Name _____

1. Kim has a pup for me.

2. He can tug and run.

3. Kim has a cat for you.

4. She can run and have fun.

Read each sentence. **1.** Draw a line under the words *has* and *for*. **2.** Draw a line under the word *he*. **3.** Draw a line under the words *has* and *for*. **4.** Draw a line under the word *she*.

6 Unit 5
Review *for, he, she, has*

At Home: Print each of the four Review Words on a card.
Take turns reading them and using them in sentences.

1. r o ck

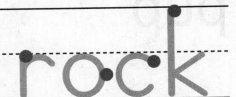

rock

2. b a g

3. b i g

4. l e g

Blend the sounds and say the word. Write the word. Draw a line under the picture that goes with the word.

At Home: Take turns writing a secret word on a scrap of paper and hiding it in one hand. If the other person chooses the hand with the word, he or she reads it.

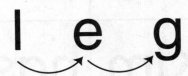

Unit 5

Review Blending with Short *a, e, i, o, u*

Name _____

Kim can run.

He is at bat.

Trace the sentences. Then write the words under their models.

4 Unit 5
Handwriting Review

At Home: Have the child draw a picture of someone who can run and someone at bat. Label each picture.

Name _____

I fed a duck.

A bug bit me.

Trace the sentences. Then write the words under their models.

At Home: Have the child draw his or her favorite animal.
Help the child label it: *I have a ____*.

Unit 5
Handwriting Review

4

McGraw-Hill School Division

Name _____

1.

2.

3.

4.

Look at the pictures in each row. Draw a circle around the picture that shows something that happened in "A Pup and a Cat." Then use the pictures you circled to retell the story.

Unit 5
Review Summarize

At Home: Take turns telling about a funny event you both experienced.

Name _____

1.

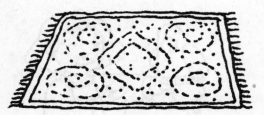

rub rug

_____

- - - - - - - - - - - - - - - - -

rug

_____

2.

Rick rid

_____

- - - - - - - - - - - - - - - - -

_____

3.

peg pig

_____

- - - - - - - - - - - - - - - - -

_____

4.

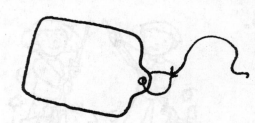

tan tag

_____

- - - - - - - - - - - - - - - - -

_____

Look at the picture. Read the words. Draw a line under the word that goes with the picture. Write the word.

At Home: Draw a ladder with four rungs. Write the letters *ap* on each rung. Climb the ladder together by saying a word that ends with *ap* as you get to each rung (*cap*, *rap*, *lap*, *nap*). Repeat with *ub*, *ock*, and *et*.

Unit 5

Review Blending with Short *a*, *e*, *i*, *o*, *u*

Name _____

1.

has •   • for

2.

for •   • she

3.

she •   • he

4.

he •   • has

Say each word. Draw a line from each word on the left to the same word on the right.

Unit 5
Review *for, he, she, has*

At Home: Write the four Review words on cards. Have the child guess the word from your clues–for example, the word has three letters, has an *s* at the end, and so on.

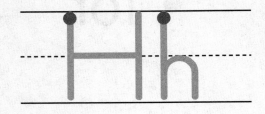

Name _____

I.

2.

3.

Write the letters *Hh*. Say the word that names each picture. Color the picture whose name begins with the same sound as *hen*.

At Home: Together, think of words that name things that begin with /h/. Have the child draw a picture of one of these things.

Unit 6
Introduce Initial /h/ h

Name _____

Find the circles in the picture. Color them yellow. Find the triangles in the picture. Color them blue.

26 Unit 6
Review Shapes: Circle, Triangle

At Home: Take turns finding circular shapes in several rooms: door knobs and cup rims. Then find square and triangular shapes: sandwiches, roofs, and kites.

Hh

Name _____

Trace the letters *Hh*. Say the word that names each picture. Color each picture whose name begins with the same sound as *hen*. Draw a line from these pictures to the letters *Hh*.

At Home: Play "Hurrah for H." Make picture cards of these and other objects. Take turns picking a card and saying "Hurrah" if the picture name begins with /h/.

Name _____

1.

2.

3.

Look at the first picture in each row. Circle the picture that shows why it happened.

Unit 6
Introduce Cause and Effect

At Home: Ask, *Why do we tie our shoes? What would happen, or could happen, if we didn't tie them?*

Name _____

1.

h   t

2.

3.

4.

Say the picture name. Write the letters that stand for the beginning and ending sounds in each picture name.

McGraw-Hill School Division

At Home: Ask the child to find which word on this page both begins and ends with the same sound (*bib*).

Unit 6
Review /h/h, /b/b

8

Name _____

1. My pup can run
with me.

2. My pup can dig
with me.

3. My pup can sit
with me.

4. I have fun with
my pup.

Read the sentence. Then draw a line under the word *with* in the sentence.

McGraw-Hill School Division

Unit 6
Introduce High-Frequency Words: *with*

At Home: Have the child draw a picture of him- or
herself playing with a friend. Help the child label
the picture *I have fun with* _____.

Name _____

1. h e n

hen

2. h u t

3. h o p

4. h i d

Blend the sounds and say the word. Write the word. Draw a line under the picture that goes with the word.

At Home: Write *hop*. Take turns changing *hop* to *hip*.
Change *hip* to *dip*. Change *dip* to *rip*. Together, decide if you made real words.

Unit 6

Review Blending with Short *a, e, i, o, u*

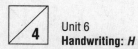

Name _____

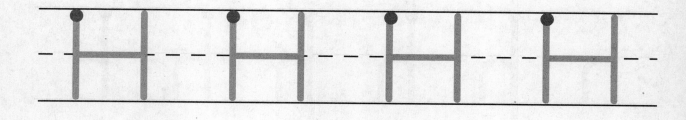

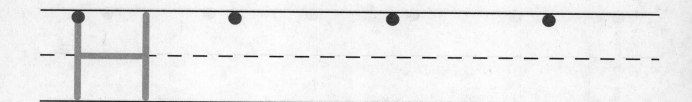

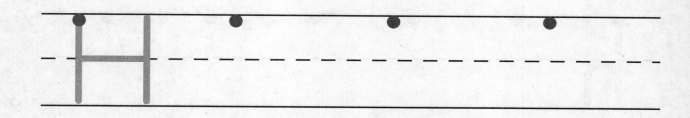

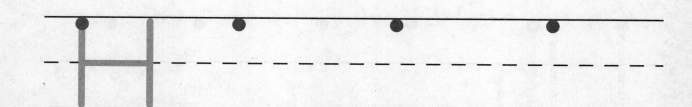

Trace and write capital *H*. Start at the dot.

4 Unit 6
Handwriting: *H*

At Home: As you both practice writing *H*, watch for any
difficulty the child may have forming the parallel vertical lines.

Name _____

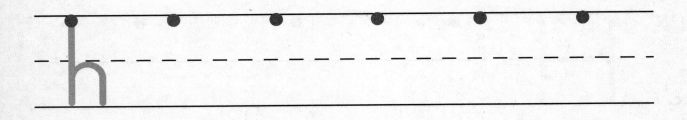

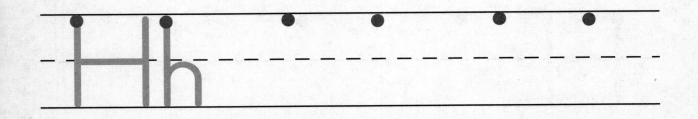

Trace and write lowercase *h*. Start at the dot. On the last line, trace and write *Hh*.

McGraw-Hill School Division

At Home: As you both practice writing *Hh*, watch that the child makes the curve in lowercase *h* on the right side of the letter.

Unit 6
Handwriting: *H, h*

Name _____

1.

2.

3.

Look at the first picture in each row. Circle the picture that shows why it happened.

3 Unit 6
Review Cause and Effect

At Home: Have the child turn the lights off and then on again. Tell what happened first. *It got dark because you turned the lights off.* Have the child tell why it got light again.

Name _____

1.

hug ham

hug

2.

hot hit

3.

bet pet

4.

ham hum

Look at the picture. Read the words. Draw a line under the word that goes with the picture. Write the word.

At Home: Write *h_m*. Take turns filling in the blank with *a*, *e*, *i*, *o*, and *u*. Decide which combinations make real words. Ask: *Which word is like singing?*

Unit 6 / **8**
Review Blending with Short *a*, *e*, *i*, *o*, *u*

316

Name _____

1. and	said	(and)
2. with	with	that
3. me	we	me
4. go	do	go
5. the	the	that

Say the first word in the row. Draw a circle around the word where you see it in the same row.

 Unit 6
Review with, go, the, me, and

At Home: Take two story books and see how many of these Review Words you can find. Which book has the greater number of Review Words?

Ww   Name _____

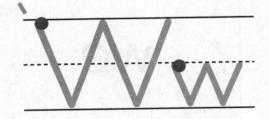

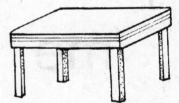

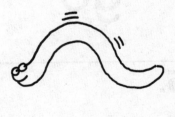

Trace the letters *Ww*. Say the word that names each picture. Color each picture whose name begins with the same sound as *wagon*. Draw a line from these pictures to the letters *Ww*.

At Home: Play a "w" riddle game. Give clues that will help identify "w" words, such as: *Which one of these do you open to get fresh air? Which one gives you fresh water?*

Unit 6
Introduce Initial /w/w   9

McGraw-Hill School Division

Name _____

Find the squares in the picture. Color them one color. Find the rectangles in the picture. Color them another color.

12 Unit 6
Review Shapes: Square, Rectangle

At Home: Ask the child to draw his or her own fantasy playground, using squares and rectangles and different colors in the drawing.

McGraw-Hill School Division

Ww   Name _____

1.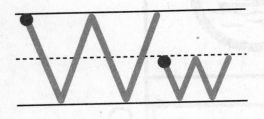

2.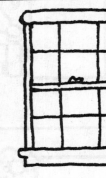

3.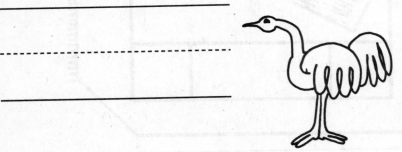

Write the letters *Ww.* Say the word that names each picture. Color each picture whose name begins with the same sound as *wagon.*

At Home: Together, find some other words that begin with *w.*
Have the child draw a picture of his or her choice.

Unit 6
Review Initial /w/w 6

Name _____

1.

2.

3.

Look at the picture on the left. Color the ☺ if the picture shows something that is good for the earth. Color the ☹ if the picture shows something that is not good for the earth.

 Unit 6
Introduce Make Inferences

At Home: Ask the child why people brush their teeth. Take turns giving examples of good and bad health habits. Smile for the good; frown for the bad.

McGraw-Hill School Division

 Name _____

1. h

w

2. h

w

3. h

w

4. h

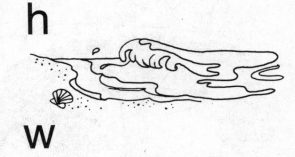

w

5. h

w

6. h

w

Say the name of each picture. Draw a circle around the letter that stands for the sound you hear at the beginning of each picture name.

At Home: Take turns drawing pictures that begin with /w/ or /h/. One person draws a picture and the other person guesses. Then switch roles.

Unit 6
Review /w/w, /h/h
6

Name _____

1. The cat was on the mat.

2. The cub was in the tub.

3. The hen was in the pen.

4. The bug was on the rug.

Read the sentence. Then draw a line under the word *was* in the sentence.

Unit 6
Introduce High-Frequency Words: *was*

At Home: Show the child the sentence starter *I was*. Then take turns finishing the sentence with words or pictures.

Name _____

1. w e t

w e t

2. w i g

3. h u t

4. w a g

Blend the sounds and say the word. Write the word. Draw a line under the picture that goes with the word.

At Home: Write _ag and _ig on cards. Take turns combining them with initial letters w, r, and t to create words. Is any combination not a word?

Review Blending with Short a, e, i, o, u

Unit 6

8

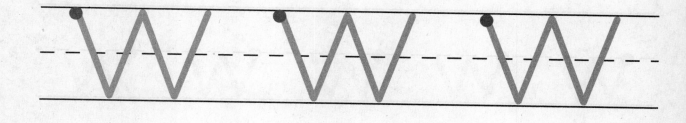

Name _____

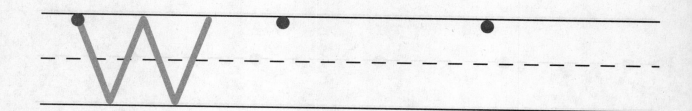

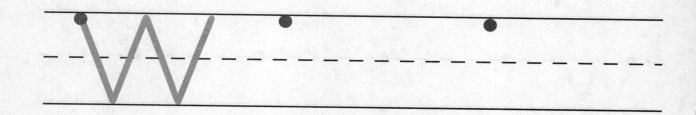

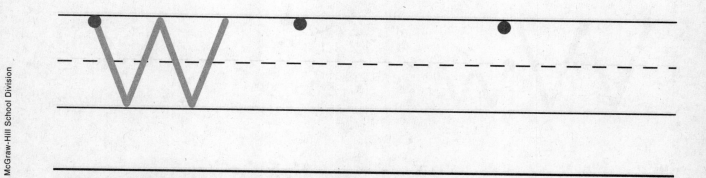

Trace and write capital *W*. Start at the dot.

4 | Unit 6
Handwriting: *W*

At Home: As you both practice writing *W*, point out to the child that *W* is almost like *M*, only upside down.

Name _____

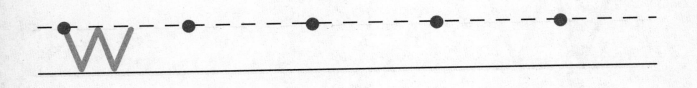

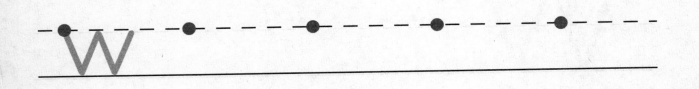

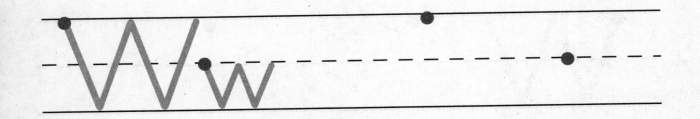

Trace and write lowercase *w*. Start at the dot. On the last line, trace and write *Ww*.

McGraw-Hill School Division

At Home: As you both practice writing *Ww*, help the child realize that the lowercase *w* is exactly the same as capital *W*, except for size.

Unit 6
Handwriting: *W, w*

4

Name _____

I.

2.

3.

Look at the picture on the left. Color the face that shows how the person in the picture might be feeling.

McGraw-Hill School Division

 Unit 6
Review Make Inferences

At Home: Tell about something that you experienced today. Then draw a face to show how you felt about it. Have the child do the same. Repeat as long as the child stays interested.

Name _____

1.

pin   win

_____

2.

hum   ham

_____

_ _ _ _ _ _ _ _ _ _ _ _ _ _ _ _ _

_____

3.

bed   wed

_____

_ _ _ _ _ _ _ _ _ _ _ _ _ _ _ _ _

_____

4.

lit   lock

_____

_ _ _ _ _ _ _ _ _ _ _ _ _ _ _ _ _

_____

Look at the picture. Read the words. Draw a line under the word that goes with the picture. Write the word.

At Home: Write *ed*. Take turns writing under it words that end with *ed*. (*bed, red, fed, wed, Ted, led, Ned*)

Unit 6   8

Review Blending with Short *a, e, i, o, u*

Name _____

1.

sit   he   (she)

2.

in   I   is

3.

was   he   with

Read the words in each row. **1.** Draw a circle around the word *she*. Draw a line under the word *he*. **2.** Draw a circle around the word *I*. **3.** Draw a circle around the word *with*. Draw a line under the word *was*.

5 Unit 6
Review *was*, *with*, *I*, *he*, *she*

At Home: Write these sentence starters and take turns finishing each one aloud: *I was with ___. She was with ___. He was with ___.*

Name _____

1.

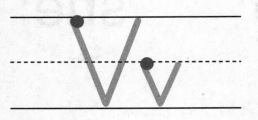  

2.

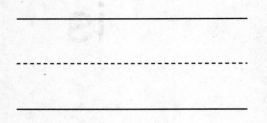  

3.

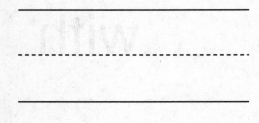  

Write the letters *Vv*. Say the word that names each picture. Color the picture whose name begins with the same sound as *vest*.

At Home: Take turns finding and saying other words that begin with *v*.

Unit 6
Introduce Initial /v/v 6

Name _____

1.

 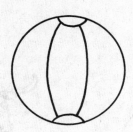 

2.

3.

4.

Look at the pictures in each row. Color all the items that belong together. Cross out the one that does not belong.

16 Unit 6
Review Categories

At Home: Gather different kitchen items or foods together. Have the child put the items in categories such as silverware, pots, vegetables, and so on.

_X

Name _____

1.

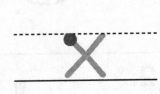

2.

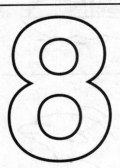

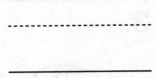

3.

Say the name of each picture in each row. Color the picture whose name has the same ending sound as *box*. Write the letter *x*.

At Home: Together, think of other words (*ax, fix,* and so on) that end in *x*. Ask the child to write *x* for each word you think of.

Unit 6
Introduce Final /ks/x

Name _____

1.

2.

3.

Look at the first picture in each row. Circle the picture that shows why it happened.

Unit 6
Review Cause and Effect

At Home: Reread a favorite story together. Take turns telling why events happened.

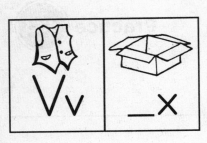

Name _____

1.

Ⓥ   X

2.

V   X

3.

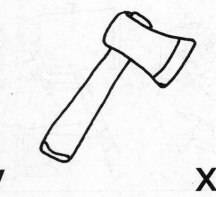

V   X

4.

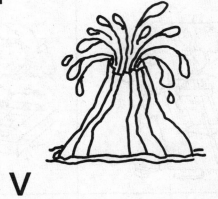

V   X

5.

V   X

6.

V   X

Say the name of each picture. Draw a circle around the *v* if it is the beginning sound (as in *vest*). Draw a circle around the *x* if it is the ending sound (as in *box*).

At Home: Together, make cards of words that begin with *v* and words that end with *x*. Practice reading and saying them.

Unit 6
Review Initial /v/v, Final /ks/x

 6

Name _____

1.

My cat is not on the mat.

2.

My cat is not big.

3.

My cat is not tan.

4.

That is not my cat!

Read the sentence. Then draw a line under the word *not* in the sentence.

McGraw-Hill School Division

Unit 6
Introduce High-Frequency Words: *not*

Name _____

1. b o x   **2.** v e t

box

3. p a n   **4.** s i x

Blend the sounds and say the word. Write the word. Draw a line under the picture that goes with the word.

At Home: Make word cards for *box, fox, vet, wet, pan, tan, six, fix.* Turn the cards facedown and take turns turning them over to find rhyming word pairs.

Unit 6   8
Review Blending with Short *a, e, i, o, u*

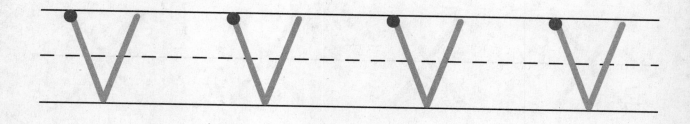

Name _____

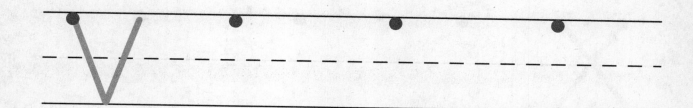

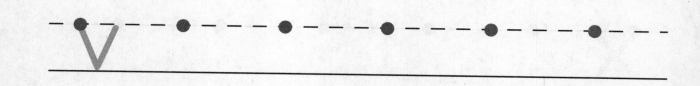

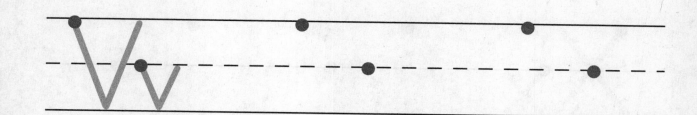

Trace and write capital *V* and lowercase *v*. Start at the dot. On the last line, trace and write *Vv*.

4 Unit 6
Handwriting: *V, v*

At Home: As you both practice writing *Vv*, check to see that the child has enough control over how wide to make the letter.

Name _____

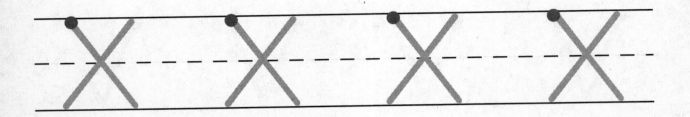

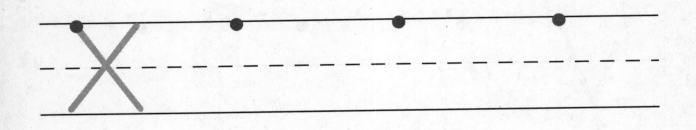

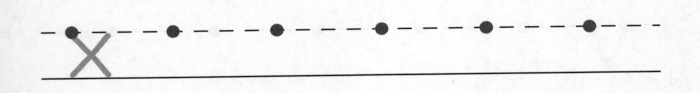

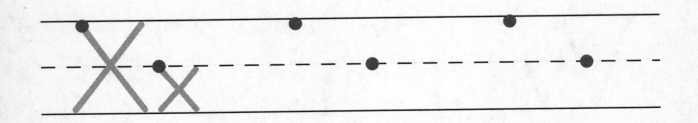

Trace and write capital *X* and lowercase *x*. Start at the dot. On the last line, trace and write *Xx*.

At Home: As you both practice writing *Xx*, be sure that the child doesn't confuse *Xx* with *Tt*.

Unit 6
Handwriting: *X, x*

4

338

Name _____

1.

2.

3.

Look at the first picture in each row. Circle the picture that shows why it happened.

Unit 6
Review Cause and Effect

At Home: Take turns making up parts of a story. Have the child begin with a character. *One day a big purple dinosaur…* Then you pick it up with a few sentences using the words *why* and *because* when appropriate. Then the child continues and so on.

Name _____

1.

hat hut

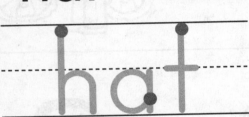

hat

2.

web wed

3.

hip rip

4.

fix fox

Look at the picture. Read the words. Draw a line under the word that goes with the picture. Write the word.

At Home: Write *ha_, we_, hi_*. Take turns creating words by ending them with the letter *d* (*had, wed, hid*). Then try the letter *t* (*hat, wet, hit*). Use the words in sentences.

Unit 6

Review Blending with Short *a, e, i, o, u*

 8

Name _____

1. "Is the pup with you?" said Mom.

2. The pup was not with Kim and Tom.

3. "We do not have the pup," said Kim.

4. "Dad and Ben are with the pup," said Tom.

Read each sentence. **1.** Draw a line under the words *is* and *with*. **2.** Draw a line under the words *was* and *not*. **3.** Draw a line under the words *we* and *do*. **4.** Draw a line under the word *are*.

Unit 6
Review *not, was, is, do, we, are, with*

At Home: Write each of the seven Review Words on two sets of paper strips. Place the strips facedown and take turns finding matching pairs.

Qq Name _____

1. Qu qu

2.

3.

Write the letters *Qu/qu*. Say the word that names each picture. Listen for the sound at the beginning of the word. Color the picture whose name begins with the same sound as *quilt*.

At Home: Together, make a paper "quilt" of letter cards. Ask the child to write *Q* or *q* on some of the cards.

Unit 6
Introduce Initial /kw/qu

Name _____

1.

 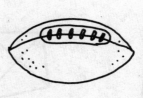 

2.

3.

4.

Look at the pictures in each row. Color all the items that belong together. Cross out the one that does not belong.

 16 Unit 6
Review Categories

At Home: Have child sort toys into categories such as puzzles, cars, blocks, art materials, and so on. Label each category with an index card.

343

Name _____

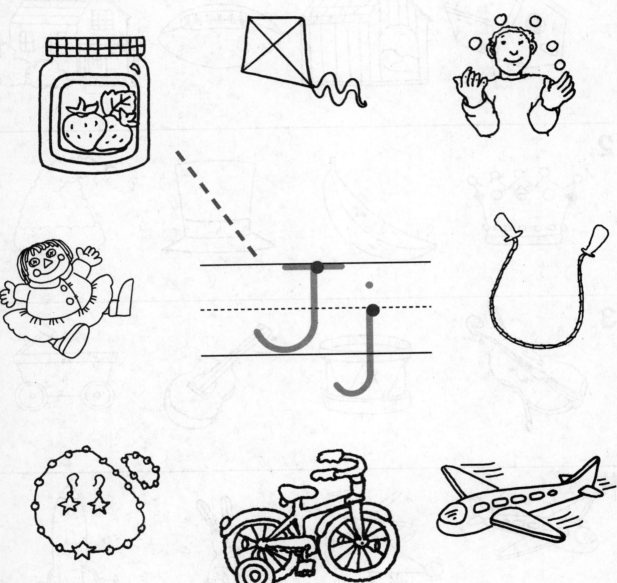

Trace the letters *Jj*. Say the word that names each picture. Color each picture whose name begins with the same sound as *jam*. Draw a line from these pictures to the letters *Jj*.

At Home: Find more /j/j words together. Which are action words? (*jog, jump*) Which are things? (*jay, jet*)

Unit 6
Introduce Initial /j/j

Name _____

1.

2.

3.

Look at the picture on the left. Then look at the two pictures on the right. Draw a line to the picture that shows where the people in the pictures are going.

Unit 6
Review Make Inferences

At Home: Talk together about things you wear or carry when you go to a particular place.

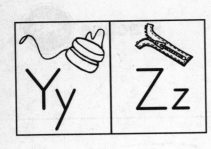

Name _____

1. y

z

2. y

z

3. y

z

4. y

z

5. y

z

6. y

z

Say the name of each picture. Draw a circle around the letter that stands for the sound you hear at the beginning of each picture name.

At Home: Make letter cards with *y* and *z*. Take turns picking a card and saying a word that begins with the letter picked.

Name _____

1.

I have a box of wax.

2.

You have a pot of jam.

3.

He has a pack of gum.

4.

She has a tin of ham.

Read the sentence. Then draw a line under the word *of* in the sentence.

Unit 6
Introduce High-Frequency Words: *of*

At Home: Have the child think of things that come in a box. Then have the child draw a picture of one thing and help him or her label it *I have a box of ____*.

Name _____

1. qu a ck

quack

_____

_____

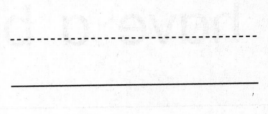

2. j u g

_____

- - - - - - - - - - - - - - - - -

_____

3. y a k

_____

- - - - - - - - - - - - - - - -

_____

4. Z a ck

_____

- - - - - - - - - - - - - - - -

_____

Blend the sounds and say the word. Write the word. Draw a line under the picture that goes with the word.

At Home: Have the child write and then read words. Give clues such as "I'm thinking of a word that begins with *y*. The next letter is *a*. The last letter is *k*. What's my word?"

Unit 6

Review Blending with Short *a, e, i, o, u*

348

Name _____

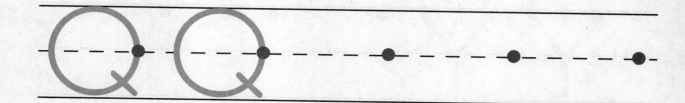

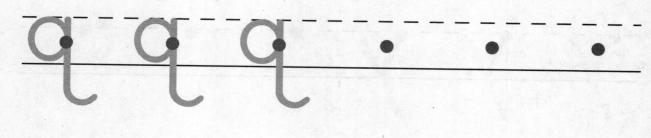

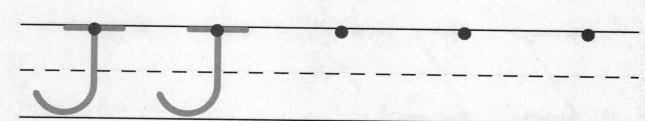

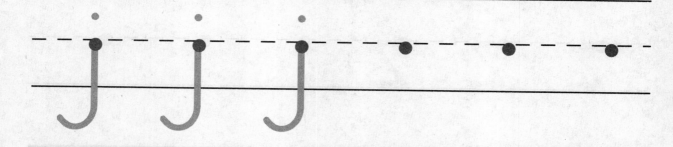

Trace and write capital *Q* and lowercase *q*, then capital *J* and lowercase *j*. Start at the dot.

4 Unit 6
Handwriting: *Q, q; J, j*

At Home: Watch as the child practices lowercase *q*. Difficulties may arise depending on whether the child makes the circle to the left or to the right.

McGraw-Hill School Division

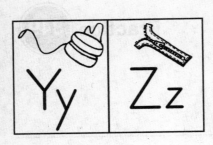

Name _____

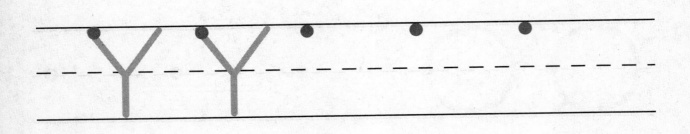

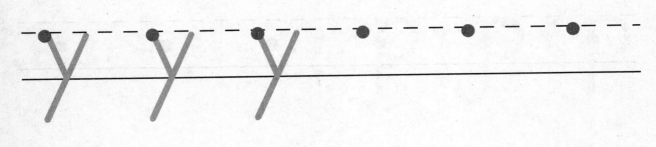

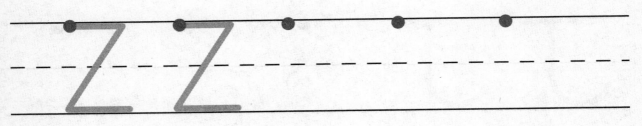

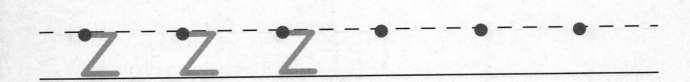

Trace and write capital *Y* and lowercase *y*, then capital *Z* and lowercase *z*. Start at the dot.

At Home: As you practice writing capital *Y* and lowercase *y* together, watch to see if the child slants the lower part of lowercase *y* correctly.

Unit 6
Handwriting: *Y, y; Z, z*

Name _____

1.

2.

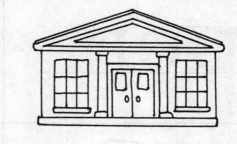

3.

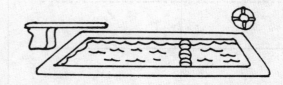

Look at the picture on the left. Then look at the two pictures on the right. Draw a line to the picture that shows where the people in the pictures have been.

Unit 6
Review Make Inferences

At Home: Play "Where Am I Going?" Take turns giving clues such as *I am wearing my bathing suit and my floater vest. I am walking on sand. Where am I going?*

Name _____

1.

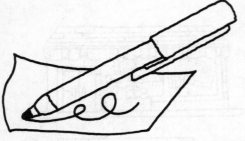

pen quick

2.

ox wax

3.

yam ham

4.

ax jug

Look at the picture. Read the words. Draw a line under the word that goes with the picture. Write the word.

At Home: Make cards for *a, e, i, o, u* and hide them in a room. Have the child look for them. When one is found, you say a word that uses the selected letter (e.g., *cat, net, pig, pot, sun*). When all five cards are found, switch roles.

Unit 6

Review Blending with Short *a, e, i, o, u*

Name _____

1. not	(not) that
2. my	me my
3. of	for of
4. that	that hat

Say the first word at the beginning of each row. Draw a circle around the word where you see it in the same row.

Unit 6
Review *of, not, that, my*

At Home: Make two sets of word cards for the words *not, my, of,* and *that.* Play a matching game and read each pair of words as you play.

Name _____

1. b u g

bug

2. j e t

 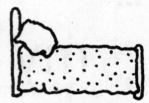

3. J a ck

4. f o x

Blend the sounds and say the word. Write the word. Draw a line under the picture that goes with the word.

McGraw-Hill School Division

At Home: Write _ick. Take turns writing under it words that end with ick (kick, lick, nick, Nick, pick, quick, Rick, sick, tick, wick).

Unit 6
Review Blending with Short a, e, i, o, u   **8**

Name _____

1.

2.

  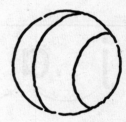

3.

Draw a circle around the *fish*. Draw a triangle around the *toy*. Draw a square around the *child*.

Unit 6
Review Shapes and Categories

At Home: Together, find objects that can be grouped into categories (things to read, things to wear, things to eat). Then look for shapes to see if any of the items contain circles, squares, triangles, or rectangles.

Name _____

1. m o p

mop

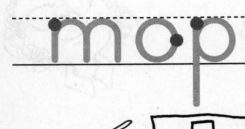

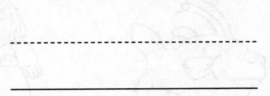

2. z i p

3. j a m

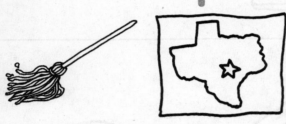

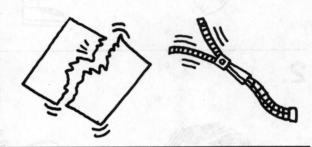

4. s u n

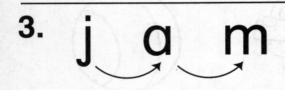

Blend the sounds and say the word. Write the word. Draw a line under the picture that goes with the word.

At Home: Write *zip*. Ask the child to change *zip* to *zap*. Write *mop*. Ask the child to change *mop* to *map*, *jam* to *Jim*, and *fix* to *fox*. Use each word in a sentence.

Unit 6
Review Blending with Short *a, e, i, o, u*

McGraw-Hill School Division

8

Name _____

1.

2.

3.

Look at the first picture in each row. Circle the picture that shows why it happened.

McGraw-Hill School Division

Unit 6
Review Cause and Effect

At Home: Talk about something that happened. Ask the child why it happened. Guide his or her answer where necessary.

Name _____

1.

pup pad

_____

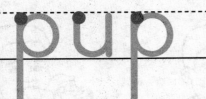 pup

2.

yet jet

_____

_____

3.

ox mix

_____

_____

4.

pick sick

_____

_____

Look at the picture. Read the words. Draw a line under the word that goes with the picture. Write the word.

At Home: Write words that end with x. Say each word before you write it. (*fix, ax, fox, ox, mix, box, six, wax*) Which of them rhyme?

Unit 6

Review Blending with Short *a, e, i, o, u*

Name _____

1.

was   (with)   of

2.

of   with   not

3.

with   not   was

4.

of   not   with

Read the words in each row. **1.** Draw a circle around the word *with*. **2.** Draw a circle around the word *of*. **3.** Draw a circle around the word *was*. **4.** Draw a circle around the word *not*.

 Unit 6
Review *with*, *was*, *not*, *of*

At Home: Print the Review Words on cards. Place cards face up on a table. Take turns removing one card and guessing which word is missing.

Name _____

1.

bat bet

<u>bat</u>

2.

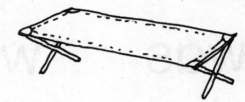

cot cut

3.

vet van

4.

wax win

Look at the picture. Read the words. Draw a line under the word that goes with the picture. Write the word.

At Home: Give clues for the child to write a word such as "This word begins with the letter *v*. The next letter is *a*. It means a kind of truck" (*van*).

Unit 6

Review Blending with Short *a, e, i, o, u*

8

Name _____

Jim had a sip.

He said, "Yum!"

Trace the sentences. Then write the words under their models.

4 Unit 6
Handwriting Review

At Home: Ask the child to tell you the name of the mark at the end of the first sentence (a period) and the mark after the word *Yum* in the second sentence (an exclamation mark). Why was each mark used?

Name _____

It was hot.

I did not jog.

Trace the sentences. Then write the words under their models.

At Home: Together, say the alphabet. Ask the child which letters are easy and which are difficult to write. Ask the child to write a letter and tell why it is easy or difficult.

Unit 6
Handwriting Review 4

Name _____

1.

2.

3.

Look at the picture on the left. Then look at the two pictures on the right. Draw a line to the picture that shows where the people in the pictures are coming from.

 Unit 6
Review Make Inferences

At Home: Talk with the child about community service. What happens when people work together for the good of others?

Name _____

1.

bed but

_____

bed

2.

hot hop

_____

3.

led leg

_____

4.

quack ax

_____

Look at the picture. Read the words. Draw a line under the word that goes with the picture. Write the word.

At Home: Change one sound/letter combination at a time as you go from *quack* to *duck*. Write *quack*. Have the child change *quack* to *tack*. Change *tack* to *tuck* and *tuck* to *duck*.

Unit 6

Review Blending with Short *a, e, i, o, u*

8

McGraw-Hill School Division

Name _____

1.

Dot, the pup, was not with Mom.

2.

Dot was with Jim and Nan.

3.

Jim, Nan, and Dot had a lot of fun.

Read the sentence. **1.** Draw a line under the words *was* and *not*. **2.** Draw a line under the word *with*. **3.** Draw a line under the word *of*.

4 Unit 6
Review *with*, *was*, *not*, *of*

At Home: Play "What Word Am I?" Give each other clues for the words *with*, *was*, *not*, and *of*. *I begin with* w *and end with* th *or I rhyme with* lot (*with, not*).

Aa Bb Cc Dd

Ee Ff Gg Hh

Ii Jj Kk Ll

Mm Nn Oo Pp

Qq Rr Ss Tt

Uu Vv Ww

Xx Yy Zz

366